Tapping into Hidden Human Capital

How Leading Global Companies Improve their Bottom Line by Employing Persons with Disabilities

DEBRA RUH

ISBN: 978-0-5781-7753-3 (sc)
ISBN: 978-0-5781-7878-3 (e)

Library of Congress Control Number: 2016907996

Rev. date: 5/31/2016

About G3ict

G3ict – the Global Initiative for Inclusive Information and Communication Technologies – is an advocacy initiative launched in December 2006 in cooperation with the Secretariat for the Convention on the Rights of Persons with Disabilities at UNDESA. Its mission is to facilitate and support the implementation of the dispositions of the Convention on the Rights of Persons with Disabilities (CRPD) promoting digital accessibility and assistive technologies. Participating organizations include industry, academia, the public sector and organizations representing persons with disabilities.

G3ict relies on an international network of ICT accessibility experts to develop policy papers, practical tools, evaluation methods and benchmarks for States Parties, Disabled Persons Organizations (DPOs) and corporations. G3ict organizes or contributes to awareness-raising and capacity-building programs around the world, in cooperation with international organizations.

Its programs are aimed at promoting ICT accessibility in practical ways and in cooperation with all stakeholders – persons with disabilities as well as public- and private-sector organizations.

G3ict produces jointly with the International Telecommunication Union (ITU) the e-Accessibility Policy Toolkit for Persons with Disabilities (www.e-accessibilitytoolkit.org), as well as specialized reports and model policies in cooperation with ITU and UNESCO that are widely used around the world by policymakers involved in the implementation of the CRPD.

For additional information on G3ict, visit www.g3ict.org.

Contents

Tying It All Together

Foreword

From large organizations with a global footprint to entrepreneurs with a few employees, attracting and retaining the right talent is the most critical success factor for their business. And as the pace of change, competitive pressures and turnover of critical human resources create new challenges every day, an untapped and often overlooked resource are employees with disabilities, whose skills, organizational commitment and positive impact on their work environment far outweigh the small costs, if any, of accommodating them.

Many books or reports have been written about the employment of persons with disabilities from a disability rights, corporate social responsibility or macro-economic perspective. *Tapping into Hidden Human Capital: How Leading Global Companies Improve their Bottom Line by Employing Persons with Disabilities* is an outstanding compendium of practical solutions for all employers by Debra Ruh, an entrepreneur with a wealth of experience in hiring persons with disabilities. It brings evidence of the benefits of employing persons with disabilities and shows step-by-step how to successfully do so.

Over the past 10 years, G3ict has focused on promoting accessible and assistive technologies for persons with disabilities and their right to access any digital content and interface. In today's world, solutions exist for any disability situation, including in the workplace. There is no reason to consider a sensorial, physical or cognitive impairment as a barrier for an employee to be fully productive. In fact, as this book demonstrates, the upside in productivity can be significant. From hiring persons with autism who excel in programming to engineers with disabilities whose turnover is minimal in highly competitive markets, the following pages provide a clear path for businesses to improve their bottom line while contributing to the global trend toward a full inclusion of persons with disabilities in society.

Our sincere appreciation goes to Debra Ruh for bringing such fresh perspective on the employment of persons with disabilities and to the many business leaders from around the world who have agreed to share their experience in successfully *Tapping into Hidden Human Capital.*

Axel Leblois
President and Executive Director, G3ict

Acknowledgments

So many people supported and encouraged me during the writing of this book. I want to thank my precious family, my best friend and husband, Edward Ruh, our daughter and inspiration Sara Ruh, born with Down syndrome. I want to thank our gifted son Kevin Ruh and his brilliant girlfriend, Emily Ha.

I want to thank my mentor and publisher Axel Leblois for his support and unwavering commitment to this book. Many thanks to my talented editors Christine Forget-Leblois and Heather McLees Frazier and to our reviewer David Ross.

Special thanks to other consultants and members of the Ruh Global Communications team, Rosemary Musachio, Eduardo Meza-Etienne, Richard J. Streitz, and Robert Lane.

I want to thank all the leaders and corporations that provided interviews, quotes and information about their efforts with employment and disabilities inclusion. Lastly, many thanks to the world leaders who shared their stories with me.

Chapter 1
Introducing the Community of Persons with Disabilities

People with disabilities are often invisible in official statistics

—*Education for All Global Monitoring Report 2006*, UNESCO

Many people are surprised to learn just how much of the world's population is affected by a disability, and how valuable an accessible environment is to the workforce and to the global marketplace. Yet, disabilities are a normal part of life: One may be born with a disability or acquire it during his or her lifetime after an accident, health issue, act of war, natural disaster or as a result of aging. Persons with disabilities are not broken, they are like everyone else; they just have to navigate the world in a different way.

Different cultures, religions, and countries define disability differently. These different definitions can be confusing to all stakeholders, including the community of persons with disabilities, governments, associations, multinational companies, and organizations trying to support the community.

An example of this confusion is the situation of little people. In some countries, like the United States, little people are covered in definitions, but in other countries, they are not. A similar situation exists for those with mental health impairments; differing definitions, inclusions and exclusions result in these people holding different status in different countries.

A Global Breakthrough in Understanding Disability

A remarkable development occurred in 2006 when, after several years of negotiations, the United Nations completed the drafting of the Convention of the Rights for Persons with Disabilities (CRPD, also known in the disability field as The Convention). Its impact is considerable: Ten years later, 161 countries had ratified it, establishing the foundation for disability rights in many countries which did not have any disability policy or legislation.

The CRPD is based on a social model for disability. It defines Persons with Disabilities as including *"those who have long-term physical, mental, intellectual, or sensory impairments which in interaction with various barriers may hinder their full and effective participation in society on an equal basis with others."*[1]

The CRPD thus defines disability as the consequence of the interaction between an impairment that may be mental,

---

[1] Convention on the Rights of Persons with Disabilities, Art.1

cognitive, physical, sensory, emotional, developmental, or a combination of these and social and environmental barriers.

It promotes a **social model of disability** as opposed to the older **medical model of disability.** The social model of disability identifies systemic barriers, negative attitudes, and exclusion caused by society (purposely or inadvertently), indicating that society is the main contributory factor in disabling people. Physical, sensory, intellectual, or psychological variations may cause individual functional limitation or impairments, but persons with disabilities can be meaningfully included in society unless society fails to take account of and include people regardless of their individual differences.

Also important is the language used to discuss those with disabilities. **People-focused language** or **people-first language** always puts the person before the disability. Instead of "disabled people," "disabled employees," or "blind person," it is more appropriate to say "persons with disabilities," "employees with disabilities," "person who is blind." This prevents people from feeling like they are only a label.

An Evolving Perception among Businesses

Businesses perspectives on the scope of the community of Persons with Disabilities has evolved as demographics have become more comprehensive. For many years in the United States – and still today in many countries – census methodologies minimized the actual numbers of persons with disabilities by utilizing medical types of questions which most people did not respond to accurately. However, recent data collection utilizing functional definitions (things that people can or cannot do in their everyday life) rather than medical definitions, have vastly expanded the breadth and depth of data available. Those new census data also give a more realistic assessment of the number of persons living with disabilities. As a result, companies all around the world recognize the imperative to develop their capacity to market and serve persons with disabilities, senior citizens in particular. Not surprisingly, businesses in fast aging countries such as Japan or Italy tend to be more focused on those issues than others. In the mobile marketplace for instance, NTT DoCoMo, the leading Japanese operator pioneered its "Raku – Raku" mobile product line for persons with disabilities and seniors. By tailoring its products and services to different types of impairment, it acquired more than 20 million new clients since inception of the product line[2]. Similarly, banks in the United States, Canada and the United Kingdom such as Wells Fargo, ScotiaBank or Barclay's have ramped up their services for the community of persons with disabilities including seniors.

The bottom line is that companies are increasingly aware of the imperative to address this major global segment of the population. Companies also realize that they are more competitive and better positioned to meet this objective if their workforce reflects their market place:

[2] NTT DoCoMo presentation at the 2014 M-Enabling Summit

"Having a diverse workforce and an environment that fosters inclusion is critical in today's global marketplace. By reflecting the diversity of the people that consume a company's products and services, global organizations are better equipped to both understand and meet the needs of their customers in a constantly changing world. Persons with Disabilities are the world's largest minority group, and embracing diversity enables a company to discover the unique, innovative skills of this important population. Through the power of inclusion, organizations can create an opportunity for all individuals to realize their potential."

– Robyn Hendrickson, Avanade Inc., Global Diversity & Inclusion Professional, Seattle.

The Facts: Latest Demographics

- According to the 2011 World Health Organization (WHO) report, one out of seven people—approximately 15 percent of the world's population—have a disability. That is over a billion people. Nearly two hundred million of these people with disabilities have severe difficulties in functioning.

- The percentage of people with disabilities is larger than any single ethnic, racial, or cultural group. In the

United States, at 19.3 percent, the number of people with disabilities exceeds the next largest minority group— Hispanic people (14.9 percent) —by a fairly wide margin.[3]

- According to the National Organization on Disabilities, one out of three US households are impacted by disabilities.[4]

- According to the 2010 Census Bureau, the US population of persons with disabilities is 56.7 million, demographically described as being five years of age or older and non-institutionalized. This equates to 19 percent of the entire US population.[5]

- In the UK, the numbers are equally as large. CSR Europe, a European business network of corporate socially responsibility firms, estimates that 8.6 million people aged 16 and over self-identify as having a disability, which translates into 15 percent of the UK population.[6]

- An estimated thirty-nine million Europeans have a disability.[7]

---

[3] http://www.ada.gov/buisstat.htm date accessed 02/22/2015

[4] http://serviceandinclusion.org/index.php?page=basic date accessed 02/22/2015

[5] http://www.disabled-world.com/disability/statistics/us-disability-stats.php date accessed 02/22/2015

[6] http://g3ict.org/resource_center/newsletter/news/p/id_273 date accessed 02/22/2015

[7] https://euobserver.com/disability/118249 date accessed 02/22/2015

Aging

As societies age, more people will acquire disabilities. There is a global increase in chronic health conditions like cancer, diabetes, cardiovascular disease, and mental health disorders. This is particularly true in countries like Japan, Canada, and the United States, where people between ages fifty and sixty-nine— born between the years 1946 and 1964—are often referred to as "baby boomers." "The last of the baby boomers turned 50 in 2014 and there are currently over 100 million adults in the United States over the age of 50." [8]

- The population over age sixty-five is expected to rise from 15.5 percent of the EU population in 1995 to 22.4 percent by 2025.[9]

- Those over fifty years of age currently account for one-fifth of the UK population. Surprising to some, 33 percent of fifty- to sixty-year-olds now have a disability.[10]

- Many think of disabilities in extreme terms such as blindness and deafness, but it also includes others with visual or hearing impairments, along with such

---

[8] https://www.immersionactive.com/item/stats-facts/

[9] http://www.boston-ia.org/library/presentations/gribbons_presentation_2005.html date accessed 02/22/2015

[10] http://www.slideshare.net/NordeaBank/nordea-csr-report-2013 date accessed 02/22/2015

challenges as motor and cognitive impairment, who are increasingly common in our aging population.

United States Census Bureau Disability Statistics[11]

The Census Bureau breaks down data by disability type. Despite this data being US based, it can be used as an indicator of how disabilities statistics break down globally.

U.S. Census Bureau American Community Survey Prevalence of Disability for Selected Age Groups: 2005 and 2010		
Categories	2005	2010
All ages	100%	100%
With a disability	18.7	18.7
Severe disability	12.0	12.6
Aged 6 and older	100%	100%
Needed personal assistance	4.1	4.4
Aged 15 and older	100%	100%
With a disability	21.3	21.3
Severe disability	14.2	14.8
Difficulty seeing	3.4	3.3
Severe	0.8	0.8
Difficulty hearing	3.4	3.1
Severe	0.4	0.5

---

[11] American Community Survey, U.S. Census Bureau: http://www.census.gov/people/disability/publications/sipp2010.html

U.S. Census Bureau American Community Survey Prevalence of Disability for Selected Age Groups: 2005 and 2010		
Categories	2005	2010
Aged 21 to 64	100%	100%
With a disability	16.5	16.6
Employed	45.6	41.1
Severe disability	11.0	11.4
Employed	30.7	27.5
Non-severe disability	5.5	5.2
Employed	75.2	71.2
No disability	83.5	83.4
Employed	83.5	79.1
Aged 65 and older	100%	100%
With a disability	51.8	49.8
Severe disability	36.9	36.6

Caregivers Matter

Caregivers represent family, friends, and others who are emotionally connected to the person with a disability and who witness first hand the challenges and biases that persons with disabilities face daily. A study by the US Department of Education found that one in three households in the United States is affected by a disability. These "invisible" members of the disability community are already embedded in corporations across every industry. As both customers and employees, they will become key participants in your company's efforts at inclusion.

Former Walgreens Senior Vice President Randy Lewis is an example of one such individual. As the father of a child with a disability, his personal experience sparked a new work concept at Walgreens distribution centers that would not only make them run more efficiently but also offer more employment opportunities for people with disabilities. His book, *No Greatness Without Goodness: How a Father's Love Changed a Company and Sparked a Movement,* tells how Walgreens created a process that revolutionized their distribution centers and created a corporate culture of inclusion, acceptance, and empowerment towards employees and customers with disabilities.

Information Technology: A Game Changer for the Inclusion of Persons with Disabilities

Of great interest to corporations is the considerable positive impact that Information and Communication Technologies (ICT), the Internet and mobile technologies can have on their interactions with persons with disabilities as employees or customers.

This is an exciting time, with emerging new technologies and mobile computing devices enabling people of all ages and all levels of education to communicate, access to information, manage their environment through the Internet of Things with alternate modes of communications such as speech recognition, biometrics or text to speech embedded in most smartphones and tablets.

These developments open opportunities for persons with disabilities to join the workforce and help create innovative processes and solutions for their employers. Designing and delivering ICT to be fully accessible ensures all individuals can enjoy the benefits and advantages of technology and add greater value to the workforce.

Adopting an inclusive, accessible and universal design approach to technology is therefore a smart strategy for both public and private organizations wishing to proactively adjust to the future needs of this growing population. By recognizing the importance of the protection and promotion of the rights and dignity of persons with disabilities through innovative assistive technologies and accessible ICTs, corporations can better ensure the full inclusion of individuals in the workforce.

"ING is a firm supporter of human rights, with this forming the basis of our environmental and social promises. We also see human rights as being about how we treat and respect our own employees worldwide. We believe all sustainable progress is driven by people with the imagination and determination to improve their future and the futures of those around them. Therefore we aim to do business with business clients and suppliers who believe in human rights as much as we do, demonstrating a high degree of governance and responsibility.

We understand that the digital world provides a unique chance to level opportunities.

Grabbing this unique chance ING now has an accessibility team working on supporting and educating IT and product development colleagues. The team also consists of people with disabilities because we understand the innovation they bring to the team speeds up our efforts to create a barrier free world."

Jake Abma, ING, Accessibility Lead

Compliance Vs. Human Rights and Market Opportunities

While accessible ICTs and the Internet are great enablers, they can also present important challenges for corporations when accessibility requirements are not met. Corporations get sued for operating inaccessible web sites or publishing inaccessible e-book readers. This is a global trend: in China, the United Kingdom, Australia or Hungary, advocates bring cases of inaccessible web sites, telephone services, or bank ATMs to court. And in the United States, the Department of Justice is definitely increasing its pressure on large organizations to align their web sites with web accessibility standards. As the following chapters will demonstrate, corporations are at the crossroads of compliance pressures, Human Rights, Citizenship considerations and market opportunities.

Bottom-Line: Benefiting from the experience and perspectives of employees and executives with disabilities has never been as important. And employing a diverse workforce inclusive of persons with disabilities creates benefits in many ways: enhanced reputation, reduction in risk, innovation opportunities and productivity gains and most importantly, nurture a loyal, productive and innovative workforce.

Business Perspective: AT&T

Interview with Susan Mazrui, Director of Public Policy, AT&T

Why does AT&T focus on accessibility?

For AT&T, accessibility is more than just a word—it's a commitment to our customers with disabilities to provide the products and services they need to stay connected. And today, we are making it easier than ever for people of all ages, and all abilities, to do just that.

AT&T quickly learned that if we were going to change, we had to be sure that persons with disabilities were not only engaged but were also part of our employment team. If we were going to do a better job of employing persons with disabilities, we had to be sure we had an accessible process and the assistive technology and accommodation tools they need to be productive.

From working with vendors and the AT&T Advisory Panel on Access & Aging to providing alternate billing formats, we're committed to creating accessible solutions for everyone.[12]

How do you work with persons with disabilities?

AT&T has great leadership support, which makes it much easier. Plus, we directly involve individuals with disabilities in a variety of different ways to help shape our direction. We do not work with just one group, and sometimes we get conflicting messages. However, for the most part, the stronger and most important messages get through at many different levels.

We also learned that if we are going to market to them, they have to have income. Everything is interdependent; it's an ecosystem. That helped us understand the breadth of the issues, which is quite large, and we learned more through

---

[12] See G3ict White Paper on AT&T methods to involve persons with disabilities in the product cycle: http://g3ict.org/resource_center/ publications_and_reports/p/productCategory_whitepapers/subCat_ 0/id_159

trial and error and that you need to have a systemic approach—something that is going to go beyond individuals who are charismatic leaders or different organizations—to support a long-term change, and you have to have the muscle behind it.

That is the evolution behind CATO—the Corporate Accessibility Technology Office.[13] We knew that when it comes to a new product being launched, you don't want to have to go back and retrofit. It's too expensive, the solutions are never as good, and you don't get the opportunity to embrace some of the innovation that comes around from disability access.

What's the impact of those policies?

We had projects and products going through, but we did not have the muscle to say "Your product is not going to be launched." They had a deadline and upward pressures—it is a business—and if push came to shove, sometimes the accessibility was built into the third or fourth generation rather than in the beginning generation. Now, this division works

---

[13] See G3ict report on AT&T's CATO strategy as an Industry model: http://g3ict.org/resource_center/publications_and_reports/p/ productCategory_books/subCat_3/id_302

with the product teams from the beginning of the process. We provide guidance and expectations for accessibility. They do an assessment and sometimes have to tell the product teams; "You are not launching your product because it is not accessible."

Now that we have the power to stop a product from moving forward if it is not accessible, we find product teams are extremely motivated to be sure the product is fully accessible for going to launch. They are not going to put up a new website, they are not going to make a fundamental change, unless they build in accessibility.

It has now become business as usual. Through that system and the ability to check the process throughout the development lifecycle, we can provide support for the organization for developing products. We believe this is positively impacting our whole culture of product development.

How is AT&T working with industry partners to further promote accessibility?

AT&T knows that the better prepared we are as an industry, the easier it is for us so we can motivate developers of software and people who are developing apps to understand their responsibilities. It requires a very strong sense of social responsibility and a sense of needing to provide the best we can to our customers. We feel the best way we can do that is to share what we know. So that means to encourage better products and services, we encourage more employment of persons with disabilities.

Chapter 2
Global Business Case for the Employment of Persons with Disabilities

The Information Technology industry suffers from a lack of talent. If I can tap the talent of an underappreciated and underutilized segment of the workforce (people with disabilities). I can beat my competition by accessing and developing a source of talent other companies fail to recognize.

Rob Figliulo, SPR Consulting,
Chief Executive Officer

In today's competitive world, where talents are at the core of economic and business success, persons with disabilities represent an untapped source of skilled employees. Employers benefit by hiring people for their unique talents and potential contributions, regardless of disability. In today's knowledge economy, diverse skills, opinions and insights offer a competitive edge. In addition, research shows that both consumers and job candidates consider an organization's commitment to social responsibility when making decisions about where to spend money and put their talents to work.

Technology and Employability

Today's average worker is far more technology-savvy than previous generations. Younger individuals are being referred to as "digital natives." They have learned how to speak the digital language at very young ages with apps, video games, tablets, smartphones, and the Internet.

Persons with disabilities have also benefited from this digital age. The reasons are simple. As technology becomes more accessible, this part of the population has mastered new digital tools and become digitally savvy. Advances in Assistive Technology (AT) and Information and Communications Technology (ICT) have improved accessibility, which has been liberating for many persons with disabilities. AT encompasses many devices developed to help individuals with disabilities perform tasks that might otherwise be difficult or impossible for them to achieve.

"Successful companies that recognize the benefits of diversity will always want to make efforts to recruit and retain people with disabilities: A disability-friendly organization that makes inclusive practice business as usual, not only benefits from recruiting from the widest possible pool of talent but, as numerous studies

have shown, will also suffer less employee churn. Ensuring that your organization has policies to support individuals has an important part to play in ensuring such success."

Neil Milliken, Head of Accessibility
& Digital Inclusion, Atos

This technology can encompass mobility devices, such as one-handed keyboards, trackball mouse, eye scanning software, wheelchairs, and electric scooters, as well as communicative equipment like hardware, software and peripherals to assist persons with visual, hearing, mobility and speech challenges. Some great examples are Voice Over or Talk Back on iPhones or Android smartphones for visually impaired persons, voice recognition for blind or physically impaired persons, or text messages and remote video sign language interpretation on demand for the deaf.

Advanced technologies such as bionic eyes and exoskeletons further expand the new frontier of AT by allowing a mother to see her child for the first time and continue to work as a programmer or allowing a teenager who injured his spine in a car accident to walk again.

The upshot of all this accessible technology is that many persons with disabilities have acquired technological skills that are transferable, valuable, and highly sought-after by employers. Most often, persons with disabilities have also learned how to self-accommodate. These skills help make them ideal candidates for employment in any company or organization.

Workplace Inclusion

Hiring a diverse workforce that includes people with disabilities allows companies to tap into this idle powerful human potential. It also allows the companies to better understand and ensure this human capital is sustained in its workforce. Hiring persons with disabilities will enable a firm to not only broaden its workforce but also have a deeper understanding of meeting its clients' needs.

> *"If persons with disabilities want to work, they must be persistent because they probably won't get hired immediately. Like any other applicant, they should tell employers what they can do and highlight their achievements. If they need some kind of accommodation, such as special software, they should explain how it would help them do the job better. I have become employed in full-time positions, which has allowed me to become self-sufficient enough to not rely on Social Security anymore. So individuals with disabilities shouldn't give up on themselves. With patience and perseverance, they can reach for stars and actually get one or two."*

Rosemary Musachio

Unrecognized Market Opportunities

Persons with disabilities are gaining legal equality in education, employment, and accessibility. The next evolutionary step is recognizing and marketing to persons with disabilities and their friends and caregivers as consumers. Millions of persons with disabilities regularly travel, shop, go to school, and eat out with family and friends.

- The large and growing market of people with disabilities has almost twice the spending power of teens, and more than *17 times the spending power* of tweens (8-12-year-olds), the two demographics most sought-after by business marketing efforts. [14]

- *WE* magazine, a lifestyle publication for people with disabilities, says people with disabilities spend $700 billion per year on technology. [15]

- A 2015 study by "Open Doors Organization" estimated that American adults with disabilities now spend $17.3 billion annually on just their own travel. [16]

- Marketing studies of the 1996 Atlanta Paralympics reveal that even households with no disability connection felt goodwill toward companies that included people with

---

[14] http://www.ada.gov/buisstat.htm date accessed 02/22/2015

[15] http://www.ada.gov/buisstat.htm date accessed 02/22/2015

[16] http://www.opendoorsnfp.org

disabilities in advertising, and were also more likely to buy their products.[17]

- The National Captioning Institute recently found that 66 percent of viewers of captioned TV are more likely to buy a product that has a captioned commercial, 53 percent will actively seek out products advertised with captions, and 35 percent will switch to brands that use captioned ads. [18]

> *"Every company states their most valuable asset is their human capital. Diversity in thought and experience identifies opportunities, solves problems faster and fosters greater creativity. Yet, the majority of global companies have not tapped into the talents of people with disabilities — even though data has (long ago) proven the benefits realized by employing people with disabilities (e.g. Greater tenure, lower absenteeism, improved culture). In short, Disability Employment is the last frontier in diversity and inclusion and it is time this issue becomes a priority for every company."*

Meg O'Connell, President,
Global Disability Inclusion

---

[17] Solutions Marketing Group, 2003
[18] http://www.ada.gov/buisstat.htm access 02/22/2015

Consumer attitudes toward companies that hire individuals with disabilities were assessed through a national public survey in the U.S. In a poll funded by the Department of Education NIDRR[19], 92 percent of consumers felt more favorable toward those that hire individuals with disabilities. The participants also had strong positive beliefs about the value and benefits of hiring people with disabilities, with 87 percent "specifically agreeing that they would prefer to give their business to companies that hire individuals with disabilities."[20]

This last statement has personal significance to me. Our daughter Sara was born with Down syndrome, and both my parents became disabled later in life. I notice which companies make their entrances accessible, if their website is accessible, whether they use individuals with disabilities in their marketing campaigns, and other efforts that may be made to include or not include my family members with disabilities. I remember shopping in Kohl's one holiday season and they had a mannequin in a wheelchair. It made me proud to shop at Kohl's.

I also chose to change pharmacies after a 20-year relationship with a retail pharmacy company in the United States, because they *did little to nothing to include persons with disabilities* in their marketing and employment efforts. Plus, their website was terribly inaccessible to many of

---

[19] www.worksupport.com/documents/romano_siperstein.pdf

[20] Journal of Vocational Rehabilitation, 24(1), 3-9, Siperstein, G. N., Romano, N., Mohler, A., & Parker, R. (2006).

my friends who are blind or cannot use their hands. I was pleased with every other aspect of my shopping experience there, but I knew of Walgreens' efforts to include people with intellectual disabilities in their distribution centers.

Their success at including these individuals has benefited not only the employees with disabilities but also their company, by expanding their pool of possible hires as well as their market. They are making other efforts to ensure accessibility of their products as well, such as by adding large-print prescriptions and talking prescription bottles. As a result, *I changed my buying behavior to reward their efforts.* The studies cited above suggest that many other customers would do the same, given adequate information and opportunity.

> *"Our mission at Microsoft is to help people everywhere meet their full potential. Our commitment to accessibility is core to who we are – it's a first-class service in every product that we ship, and a set of investments we continue to grow year after year, product after product. Quite simply, making the computer easier to see, hear, and use is what we're all about."*
>
> Rob Sinclair, Chief Accessibility Officer, Director of Accessibility, Microsoft

Businesses work hard to create positive brand recognition. Including persons with disabilities among your employees is an excellent way to enhance your brand image. Persons with disabilities should be viewed as a viable pool of potential employees as well as an emerging market that, together with their friends, families, and caregivers, have trillions of dollars in disposable income. Stories of successful disability inclusion within a company should be included in marketing efforts, shareholder reports, and corporate social responsibility reports.

Bottom line: Employing persons with disabilities not only expands your pool of possible talent, it is smart business.

"Over the last several decades, we have seen dramatic changes around the globe for individuals with disabilities (IWD's). They have not only become a major force in the market place, but are impacting our employment agencies through innovated mainstream products and services. Frankly, it's an advantage to employers to hire employees with disabilities. Another exciting transformation for companies hiring IWD's is the evolution of the transportation field which is one of the primary hurdles for IWD's. Affordable options like Uber have made more transportation more accessible. Next on the horizon, telepresence robots that offer an

IWD's virtual way to participate in on-site work actives or the futuristic self-driving car, embraced as a stress-reducing convenience for harried drivers and a potential advance in road safety, could also prove to be a life-changing breakthrough for many people with disabilities, granting them a new measure of employment independence."

Christopher M. Lee, Ph.D., Executive Director, AMAC Accessibility Solutions & Research Center, Georgia Institute of Technology

Understanding the Talents of Persons with Disabilities

"At Northrop Grumman, we have worked extremely hard, partnering with external and internal organizations, to raise awareness and provide career opportunities for employees from all demographic communities. Persons with disabilities have as much to offer to a prospective employer as any candidate."

Bob Vetere, Human Resource Specialist – EEO, Northrop Grumman

Employees with disabilities bring unique experiences that can help transform a workplace and enhance products and services. For instance, persons with disabilities must overcome many physical and digital accessibility barriers. We forget to make a website or intranet accessible or to tag images for screen readers. Because of these challenges, persons with disabilities often create elaborate systems and tools to help simplify their lives in creative ways. They develop a different and often stronger relationship with their employer than the average employee and come with unique technical strengths.

> *"At Barclays, we have always hired based on merit and whether or not you are the best person for the job regardless of a disability, gender, race or sexual orientation. Over recent years, we've increasingly seen clear business benefits for recruiting and retaining disabled talent and are increasingly looking at how we attract, develop, promote and retain this particular section of our colleague base. We do this through a variety of programs including our Reach colleague network, a development program for colleagues with disabilities, a workplace adjustments program and a candidate mentoring program for potential colleagues*
>
> *We've also been working hard to ensure that all our customers can access our products and services whether they be in person or through one of our digital channels as well as creating additional options for customers to*

use if our mainstream options aren't the best way of doing their business. A great example is in our branch and on the phone SignVideo virtual sign language interpreter service which allows a sign language user to interact with our colleagues instantly rather than waiting for an interpreter which could take weeks to arrange. We were the first bank in the UK to offer this service in branch and we're really proud of our history of accessibility innovation."

Paul Smyth, Head of IT
Accessibility at Barclays

As part of your team, employees with disabilities bring new ideas to the workforce, which often leads to innovation in the workplace. Let's explore a few benefits to the employer.

- SAP, which employs more than 65,000 people worldwide, sees a "potential competitive advantage to leveraging the unique talents of people with autism, while also helping them to secure meaningful employment.[21]"

- Areva, the largest nuclear engineering firm in the world, has a proactive policy to hire engineers with disabilities to promote equal employment opportunities but also to fight competition poaching their top talents: engineers

[21] Source: ABC News http://abcnews.go.com/beta/Health/Autism/tech-giant-sees-competitive-advantage-autistic-workforce/story?id=19234442

with disabilities over the long term are indeed more loyal to their organization and appreciative of their work environment, with better work ethics and less absenteeism. The outcome to Areva's bottom line is that the more engineers with disabilities, the stronger their engineering team.[22]

- When Adobe Systems invested in new developments for PhoneGap, the well- known open source multi-platform app development tool, a blind software engineer came up with the concept of an automated mobile accessibility plug-in, still the leading such tool in the marketplace.

- Cincinnati's Children hospital hired employees with intellectual disabilities, and the job coach created detailed, visual pictures for the training department. The employees with intellectual disabilities were able to learn the position in about 25 percent less time than previous employees. The employer then started using those training materials for all employees.[23]

- Many employers have found that *hiring persons with disabilities allowed them to develop and expand better business processes.* Cisco had a senior manager who broke his shoulder. He was struggling to type with a traditional keyboard so they purchased speech

---

[22] http://www.areva.com/EN/careers-409/social-and-human-responsibility-actions-and-measures-taken.html

[23] http://www.worksupport.com/research/viewContent.cfm/42

recognition software for him. The software allowed him to continue to be productive as his shoulder healed.

> *"The inclusion of PwD's into the work place provides a company with ever expanding rewards, plus allows persons of this community to continue being a valued, contributing part of society. Dr. Steven Hawking is a perfect example of this, regardless of his obvious physical limitations; his supreme hyper intelligence has arguably provided some of the most important work to Theoretical Physics our planet has seen this century. Had is intelligence not been obvious to his mentors prior to his body failing, we must wonder, would he have been given the same opportunities otherwise.*

> Richard J. Streitz, Ruh Global
> Communications, Chief Operating
> Officer, Former Disney Imagineer

- *Hiring persons with disabilities can help employers to enhance, develop, and implement management strategies to improve productivity.* Global accounting firm EY hired an accountant who was deaf. He was part of a team that met each week to discuss projects. He suggested a tool that would record and turn the meetings into text. His coworkers found that these transcriptions to be invaluable. The entire team became more efficient and productive because of this tool.

Employing persons with disabilities can also help with product and service innovation, stimulate new product and service development, and customize products and services to increase profitability across the business. One large software company asked employees with disabilities how they could design a more accessible website to meet the needs of clients with disabilities. The employees gave them examples of websites that they considered accessible and made suggestions for the redesign of the company's website. Management was delighted with many of the suggestions and had many of the ideas built into the website. The team also began to market the ideas to clients and showed how these efforts created a more beneficial experience for all customers. More clients started using the website instead of calling the customer service line, which saved the company significant money by reducing the number of customer service representatives. It also allowed the company to better use the website and cross-sell other services to the clients.

Such steps to enhance the accessibility of a company website can have dramatic positive impact on organizations. One firm found that the redesign of its website resulted in doubling the number of visitors seeking quotes and buying their financial products online. The website also reduced maintenance costs by two-thirds..[24]

---

[24] W3C case study: http://www.w3.org/WAI/bcase/legal-and-general-case-study

- Such steps to enhance the accessibility of a company web site can have dramatic positive impact on organizations: Caroline Fawcett, Legal & General customer experience director, says that after the redesign of its website, "The new site has almost doubled the number of visitors seeking quotes and buying Legal & General financial products online. It has cut maintenance costs by two-thirds and increased the amount of natural search traffic we get by half as much again."[25]

- As companies seek to diversify their workforce to better reflect their customer base, employees with disabilities bring a unique and critical perspective on customers with disabilities including among senior citizens.

  > *"At Accenture, we believe each person has unique skills, talent and strengths to contribute. Our focus is to attract, retain, develop and advance the best talent in the world. We are committed to ensuring an inclusive environment that supports our people with disabilities and provides reasonable accommodations and accessibility so they can each perform at their full potential. Creating this inclusive environment where everyone has*

---

[25] W3C case study: http://www.w3.org/WAI/bcase/legal-and-general-case-study

> *an equal opportunity to contribute is at the heart of our core values."*
>
> Nellie Borrero, Managing Director –
> Global Inclusion & Diversity, Accenture

Myths and Misconceptions

So if persons with disabilities bring such great benefits and are such wonderful employees, why are many employers reluctant to hire them?

One reason is accommodation. Whenever the issue of employing persons with disabilities arises, employers immediately think about accommodation. *Employers fear accommodations and adjustment will be expensive and difficult to implement.* The truth is that need for an accommodation depends on the nature of the disability., Accommodations are less challenging than one expects. According to studies by Job Accommodation Network, about 56 percent of employees with disabilities do not need accommodations.[26] Management at TecAccess, a consulting company specializing in ICT accessibility found this to be true. While 80 percent of its team was comprised of persons with disabilities, many of these employees did not require accommodation.

---

[26] www.askjan.org

Most of the accommodations were readily available tools like Skype chats to help employees who could not speak. Using those tools systematically to maintain an accessible work environment also made the entire team more productive.

The truth is that employers accommodate employees all the time in order to remain employers of choice. Accommodations come in many forms to include allowing an executive to take Tuesday afternoons off to coach his daughter's softball team, allowing a mother with small children to telework so she can reduce childcare costs and be more productive, or providing an employee with a broken arm a different keyboard so that he can type with one hand. For those employees who benefit from accommodations, whether they have a disability or not, those adjustments are typically inexpensive and routine. Expenditures associated with accommodations are usually a one-time expenditure costing less than $500.

When employers were polled about the paid accommodations, they felt that the initial investment in the employee paid for itself many times over in the form of reduced training costs and increased productivity.[27]

> *"The study results consistently showed that the benefits employers receive from making workplace accommodations far outweigh the*

---

[27] Source: Job Accommodation Network, 2014 "Workplace accommodation, low cost, high impact"

low cost. Employers reported that providing accommodations resulted in such benefits as retaining valuable employees, improving productivity and morale, reducing workers' training costs, and improving company diversity. These benefits were obtained with little investment. The employers in the study reported that a high percentage (58 percent) of accommodations cost absolutely nothing to make, while the rest typically cost only $500."

Louis E. Orslene, MPIA, MSW, Co-Director
of the Job Accommodation Network

Another important study from the Job Accommodation Network measured the effectiveness of accommodations. It addressed the often heard myth that accommodations are not effective. Of the employers responding to their survey they reported " ...74 percent reported the accommodations were either very effective or extremely effective".[28]

There are other reasons why so many employers have difficulty including persons with disabilities in their organizations. Hiring persons with disabilities is often seen as a compliance issue instead of a bottom-line differentiator.

---

[28] Citation for this publications is: Job Accommodation Network (Original 2005, Updated 2007, Updated 2009, Updated 2010, Updated 2011, Updated 2012, Updated 2013, Updated 2014, Updated 2015). *Workplace accommodations: Low cost, high impact.* http://AskJAN. org/media/lowcosthighimpact.html

Many employers believe that employment of persons with disabilities is difficult. Myths abound. Employers fear of direct and non-direct compliance costs that they will be required to:

- Hire people who are not qualified for their positions

- Carve up their positions

- Find additional space for job coaches

- Work with hundreds of service providers

- Retain an employee who will not perform or be as productive as their peers

Contrary to these notions, many companies have found that persons with disabilities are productive, dependable and qualified employees.

> *"I have heard some Disability Consultants in the U.S. often criticizing employers stating they are afraid to hire persons with disabilities. In my experience, that is not the issue. Employers are focused on overarching hiring compliance, with a perspective of Equal Employment Opportunity. They are not 'afraid' of any particular group over another but are nervous about the risks of non-compliance associated with all of them. Of most importance though,*

> *these employers want to create a pathway for all people into their organization, so they can hire and retain the best talent to enable their business success."*

> Kim Vanderland, Senior Vice President,
> Workplace Strategy, JLL

Hiring Persons with disabilities: What It Takes

Creating an environment in which persons with disabilities feel valued and respected is critical to successfully recruiting and retaining them. Successful workplace inclusion demands a strategy that includes companywide policies, attitudes and best practices.

These factors positively influence employee perceptions about the work environment, which, in turn, improve engagement, job satisfaction and productivity. Creating a positive work environment for employees should include strategies for the inclusion of persons with disabilities. All employees benefit when the employer creates an environment that allows them to work to their full potential.

As discussed in chapter 1, including persons with disabilities allows a company to better serve its market place by giving it an edge on understanding its diverse client base.

> *"Hiring a qualified candidate with a disability should not be done because it is the "right"*

thing to do, if we are to make progress as a country, we have to start to consider and hire from this segment because, for many reasons, it is the smart thing to do for our businesses."

Kevin Bradley, Senior Manager, Global Workforce Inclusion, The Boeing Company

So how do you accomplish these goals?

- *Focus on inclusion and accessibility as "differentiators".* Applicants, employees, and customers are increasingly seeking information and communication technology that meets their needs. Integrating accessibility/universal design standards and governance into infrastructure helps positively position an organization. Also making your data human-centric will make it more usable for all clients. Chapter 5 discusses Universal Design (UD) in more detail.

- *Focus on bottom-line benefits.* A company's reputation can be enhanced by ensuring everyone is included in your workforce and client base. Hiring persons with disabilities has many bottom-line benefits. It is not only about persons with disabilities, it is also about their families and friends, as well as social good. It is good for business to be perceived as an exemplary employer, exemplary neighbor and business, and exemplary company with innovative solutions.

"Vodafone is interested in all our customers and we are committed to assuring that our solutions are accessible to everyone, including people with disabilities. We do this because it makes good business sense and gives us a competitive advantage."

Santiago Moreno Fernandez, Director General, Vodafone Spain Foundation

Make your firm an employer of choice. These efforts help expand the pool of eligible applicants as well as helping to attract the most talented applicants. They also have the potential to increase your customer base. The global economy makes accessibility a higher priority in terms of product design given an increasingly competitive marketplace.

Improve productivity and reduce costs. Efforts to improve the accessibility and ease of use of workplace technologies improve the work environment for employees with disabilities and mature workers who acquire disabilities as they age. These efforts also attract technology-savvy younger workers who are attracted by the added functionality of workplace technology. Making technology accessible helps mitigate legal risk by providing appropriate tools both internally (employees) and externally (customers). It improves retention and reduces costs associated with training new employees.

As Thomas J. Donohue, president and CEO of the U.S. Chamber of Commerce stated in his introduction of

"Leading Practices on Disability Inclusion" with US Business Leadership Network (USBLN) Executive Director Jill Houghton, "Successful businesses recognize that incorporating disability in all diversity and inclusion practices positively impacts their companies' bottom line. Corporate CEOs understand that it's cost-effective to recruit and retain the best talent regardless of disability."[29]

"Like all STEM disciplines, technology aptitude requires minds that are creative and committed to the task, project and team. Technology also permeates every industry and company - nationally and globally. People with disabilities in the workforce are creative by nature or necessity, determined and committed to their success, and value being a productive member of a team. SPR Consulting has a long-standing commitment to supporting professionals with disabilities in the tech field. We source, support the growth of, and deploy this segment of the workforce as a competitive advantage just as we support other historically overlooked segments of our workforce."

Patrick Maher, SPR Consulting,
Director of Civic Engagement

---

[29] https://www.uschamber.com/leading-practices-disability-inclusion-0

Bottom line: Hiring a diverse workforce that includes persons with disabilities confers multiple benefits on your business without adding significant risk.

Business Perspective: COMPUTER AID, INC. (CAI)

An interview with Ernest Dianastasis, a Managing Director at Computer Aid, Inc. (CAI). CAI is located in Delaware and one of the largest IT consulting firms in the United States. Partnering with Specialisterne, a Danish social organization, CAI has created an initiative to hire individuals with autistic spectrum disorders (ASDs). Dianastasis explains how employees with autism will comprise at least 3 percent of CAI's workforce by the end of 2015: "It's about bringing highly skilled people, who have often been overlooked, into the corporate world"

Four of the individuals on the ASD spectrum were employed in IT and business process jobs at Delaware's Department of Health and Social Services. By the end of 2014, the CAI-Specialisterne collaboration trained about 50 workers, which it planned to place with their clients in two additional state government agencies, a Fortune 50 bank, a major insurance company, and with other clients.

Business Perspective: ACCENTURE

Embracing inclusion and diversity – a powerful catalyst for success. "The diversity of our people is part of what makes Accenture exceptional. We recognize that each person has unique strengths. And by embracing those strengths, we all deliver performance – together. Accenture provides an inclusive and equitable work environment for persons with disabilities and drives awareness through training programs.

We are committed to creating and providing an inclusive, open and equitable environment for individuals with different backgrounds, lifestyles, needs and expectations to be successful. To build awareness and understanding of issues faced by persons with disabilities, we sponsor networking, training and information sharing.

We also encourage the provision of reasonable accommodations—modifications or adjustments to a job or the work environment to assure that a qualified individual with a disability has rights and privileges in employment equal to those of employees without disabilities—to create an adaptable work environment. To help our people with disabilities employees obtain the accommodation they need to do their jobs, we recently developed a tool that allows people to request assistive technology online for themselves or on behalf of a colleague.

Did you know? Accenture has nearly 4,000 Persons with Disabilities (PwD) champions around the globe.

Accenture is proud to be a member of the International Labour Organization (ILO) Global Business & Disability Network (http://www. businessanddisability.org/index.php/en/about-the-network/charter), which helps advance the creation of decent work and the economic and working conditions that give working people and business people a stake in lasting peace, prosperity and progress. We recently signed a charter with ten other companies to express our commitment to promoting and including persons with disabilities throughout our operations worldwide.

Our geographies offer a variety of initiatives designed to support the specific needs of persons with disabilities in their area. For example, Accenture in France offers a helpline,

"Accent Sur Le Handicap," that any Accenture employee can call—anonymously and at no charge—for information and advice on disability-related topics. In India, our offices host webinars and workshops featuring motivational speakers and training on how to support the needs of Persons with Disabilities coworkers."

Change your perspective

Accenture people with disabilities, champions and allies share their perspectives on accommodations, the importance of an inclusive work environment and the power of seeing beyond a disability in our new global video for International Day of Persons with Disabilities.

Watch the video: https://www.accenture. com/us-en/company-video-library) for the transcript visit: https://www.accenture.com/ t20151214T211209__w__/us-en/_acnmedia/ PDF-2/Accenture-Change-Your-Perspective-Persons-with-Disabilities-2015-Video-Transcript.pdf

"Sin Barreras" (Without Barriers) is a workplace inclusion program developed by our colleagues in Argentina focused on creating jobs for persons with disabilities.

Watch the video: (https://www.accenture.com/us-en/company-video-library)

Another good resource is Accenture's Fact Sheet on Persons with Disabilities

https://www.accenture.com/t20151216T215606__w__/za-en/_acnmedia/PDF-1/Accenture-Persons-with-Disabilities-Fact-Sheet.pdf#zoom=50

Chapter 3
Global Trends

Global enterprises are focused on important global trends in the employment of persons with disabilities. Those include governments' eagerness to leverage the economic benefits of increasing the employment of persons with disabilities, the impact of aging on hiring requirements and policy pressures in the form of quotas from governments and the need for most countries to align with The Convention.

Let's explore these topics:

The Big Picture, Savings for Countries

Many countries have shrinking workforces due to aging, globalization, technological and communications advances. In addition to deriving benefits, organizations that hire persons with disabilities can significantly contribute to improving the economic balance of social services. KPMG conducted a study that showed the potential benefit for Spain of including persons with disabilities in the workforce.

This study focused on the impact of special employment centers (SEC) in Spain. The table below provides a detailed analysis of the financial return of SEC in 2011, in terms of the government spending in cash benefits as well as the reduction of taxes.

As shown in the table below, the employment of persons with disabilities has real benefits in reducing the tax and social support burden on all of society. For every euro contributed to the SEC program by the government, 1.43 euros were contributed back by persons with disabilities to the government budget.[30]

While the above model is specific to Spain and may not be applicable elsewhere, it still demonstrates the significant benefits for society at large of employing persons with disabilities.

---

[30] http://www.feaps.org/files/Documentos/CEEcompleto.pdf

Cost to the Government	Total Amounts (Euros)	Return of Investment on SEC	Total Amounts (Euros)	Impact
Cash Balance				
Committed expenditure for SEC	€ 323,514,020	Personal Income Tax & Social Security	€ 179,332,171	
		Value Added Tax	€ 239,555,474	
		Corporate Income Tax	€ 40,700,000	
Non-Cash Balance				
Incentive to employers:		LISMI (Non discrimination act) benefits	€ 1,778,738	
100 percent reduction of employers corporate social security contributions	€ 204,815,193	Non-contributive pensions	€ 22,730,090	
		Contributive pensions	€ 43,417,067	
		Healthcare expenditure savings	€ 97,227,989	
		Savings in occupational employment program	€ 135,389,131	
Total	€ 528,329,213		€ 760,130,661	
Net positive financial impact				**€ 231,801,448**

Impact of Aging Societies on Hiring

According to the International Labor Organization, the world population is aging rapidly. The developed countries are aging faster than the developing world; however, the developing world is only a few decades behind. China also has a rapidly aging society due to many years of one child policy. The Chinese government end the one child policy in late 2015 due to issues with an aging population. "To promote a balanced growth of population, China will continue to uphold the basic national policy of population control and improve its strategy on population development," Xinhua reported, citing a communique issued by the ruling Communist Party. "China will fully implement the policy of 'one couple, two children' in a proactive response to the issue of an aging population."

As older workers leave the workforce, it becomes critical to include all available working age persons, including those with disabilities.

- In developed countries, the number of people over the age of 65 is expected to triple in the next 40 years increasing from 5.8 percent to 15 percent of the entire population.[31]

---

[31] http://www.ilo.org/global/publications/magazines-and-journals/world-of-work-magazine/articles/WCM_041965/lang--en/index.htm

Medical Advancements are helping us live longer. Aging in developing countries is expected to increase from 16 percent to 26 percent for many reasons, including medical advancements. An increase of more than 60 percent, according to the Non-Communicable Diseases and Mental Health (NMH) report.[32]

A few examples:

- One in three people experience disabilities as they age. At age 50, adults are likely to begin experiencing age-related physical changes that may affect hearing, vision, cognition and mobility.[33]

- The Japanese population is the oldest in the world, with 22 percent of Japanese being 65 years of age or older.[34]

- Italy, Germany and parts of the United States quickly follow, with over 20 percent of their populations 65 or older.[35]

Business Perspective: ATOS

"In the Atos global diversity policy, we have a statement on disability inclusion:

---

[32] http://www.who.int/nmh/publications/ncd_report_chapter1.pdf

[33] According to the AARP (American Association of Retired Persons)

[34] **worldpopulation**review.com/countries/japan-**population**

[35] http://www.nytimes.com/2014/04/23/upshot/the-american-middle-class-is-no-longer-the-worlds-richest.html?_r=0

Our Ambition is to create an inclusive environment that makes Atos an employer of choice, enabling the organisation to attract and retain talented people with a wide range of abilities.

We recognise that employing people with disabilities furnishes us with valuable insights & different perspectives that give our organisation an innovative competitive edge. It also means we can make better connections with our customers.

We aim to give people with disabilities the best possible opportunities to fulfil their potential by:

- Increasing our workforces understanding of disability and challenging attitudes about capability and ability.

- Removing barriers:

  o In our physical environment

  o In our organisation, procedures and working practices

  o In our IT environment

- Ensuring that people with disabilities have the opportunities to fulfil their potential and realise their aspirations.

- Ensuring that the voices of people with disabilities are heard.

Atos has a strong focus on accessibility and usability. Highlights include the creation of a centre of excellence in the UK which also runs our accessibility academy programme, the adaption of our corporate colour palate to take into account accessibility in our branding and contribution to accessibility standards creation in both UK and France. Our aim is to design digital services that meet the needs of all users, including those dependent on assistive technology. To this end we have adopted ISO Accessibility standards in our Global Development Portfolio. In the UK we use the Business Disability Forum Accessibility Maturity Model to measure our progress."

Neil Milliken, Atos, Head of
Accessibility & Digital Inclusion

What does this mean for you as an employer?

These numbers dramatically impact the workforce. People are staying in the workforce longer than in the past; their reasons include financial need, benefits, exploring second career options, entrepreneurial desires, wanting to stay engaged or relevant and make a difference, and not wanting to be a burden on their families and society. As mentioned in chapter 1, many older workers will acquire disabilities as they age. Making your firm, its systems and processes accessible to workers with age-related disabilities will help cut the costs of pensions and retirement accounts, as well as of recruiting and training new employees.

The Convention on the Rights of Persons with Disabilities

In December 2006, the United Nations General Assembly adopted the text of the Convention on the Rights of Persons with Disabilities after several years of negotiation among Member States and with an extensive participation of civil society. Eighty-two countries signed it on the first day of opening for signatures, the largest number ever in history for any international treaty.

By early 2016, 160 countries had signed it and 161 have ratified it, meaning that it has the force of law in all those countries. This means that more than 80 percent of the world's population is now covered by the same policy, legal and regulatory framework for the protection of the rights of persons with disabilities.

Treaties such as The Convention take time to be enacted at country level with "progressive implementation," including adapting legislation and regulations and implementing programs. The movement toward alignment on minimum policy standards worldwide, however, is inescapable. Article 8.2.III of The Convention requires States Parties to "promote recognition of the skills, merits and abilities of persons with disabilities and their contributions to the workplace and the labor market". And while several articles of the Convention stress the obligation to promote the full inclusion of persons with disabilities in society at large and to eliminate discrimination, it is Article 27 that contains the set of guidelines that will progressively translate into policies in all countries around the world:

"Persons with disabilities add valuable contributions to the workforce and global society. They are changing the way in which the international community views persons with disabilities and their abilities. Each of us has a crucial role to play in this historical process toward the full realization of human rights and development for all. In my view, the development of international human rights instruments like the United Nations Convention on the Rights of Persons with Disabilities (CRPD) is akin to creating a new "universal language" for societies and individuals worldwide to discuss

> *the way forward in realizing the human rights of all persons, with or without disabilities."*

Ambassador Luis Gallegos

CRPD Article 27 - Work and employment

1. States Parties recognize the right of persons with disabilities to work, on an equal basis with others; this includes the right to the opportunity to gain a living by work freely chosen or accepted in a labor market and work environment that is open, inclusive and accessible to persons with disabilities. States Parties shall safeguard and promote the realization of the right to work, including for those who acquire a disability during the course of employment, by taking appropriate steps, including through legislation, to, inter alia:

(a) Prohibit discrimination on the basis of disability with regard to all matters concerning all forms of employment, including conditions of recruitment, hiring and employment, continuance of employment, career advancement and safe and healthy working conditions;

(b) Protect the rights of persons with disabilities, on an equal basis with others, to just and favorable conditions of work, including equal opportunities and equal remuneration for work of equal value, safe and healthy working conditions, including protection from harassment, and the redress of grievances;

(c) Ensure that persons with disabilities are able to exercise their labor and trade union rights on an equal basis with others;

(d) Enable persons with disabilities to have effective access to general technical and vocational guidance programs, placement services and vocational and continuing training;

(e) Promote employment opportunities and career advancement for persons with disabilities in the labor market, as well as assistance in finding, obtaining, maintaining and returning to employment;

(f) Promote opportunities for self-employment, entrepreneurship, the development of cooperatives and starting one's own business;

(g) Employ persons with disabilities in the public sector;

(h) Promote the employment of persons with disabilities in the private sector through appropriate policies and measures, which may include affirmative action programmes, incentives and other measures;

(i) Ensure that reasonable accommodation is provided to persons with disabilities in the workplace;

(j) Promote the acquisition by persons with disabilities of work experience in the open labor market;

(k) Promote vocational and professional rehabilitation, job retention and return-to-work programs for persons with disabilities.

2. States Parties shall ensure that persons with disabilities are not held in slavery or in servitude, and are protected, on an equal basis with others, from forced or compulsory labor.[36]

> *"Employment rates of persons with disabilities in some countries are as low as one third of that of the overall population.*
>
> *"An estimated 15 percent of the world's population has a disability and over two thirds of persons with disabilities live in developing countries, where the gap in primary school attendance rates between children with disabilities and others ranges from 10 percent to 60 percent.*
>
> *"This multi-dimensional exclusion represents a huge cost, not only to persons with disabilities but to society as a whole."*

Ban-Ki Moon, Secretary General,
United Nations, 2011

---

[36] http://www.un.org/disabilities/convention/conventionfull.shtml

Business Perspective:
U.S. Department of Labor

What the Office of Disability Employment Policy of the Department of Labor does in the United States

Training and Education

- Disseminating training and education materials to United States Business Leadership Network (USBLN) members on issues of concern in order to advance the recruitment and employment of job candidates with disabilities

- Disseminating and sharing effective disability employment practices and providing expertise in communicating such information to employers and employees

- Providing expertise on key industry issues as they pertain to the employment of people with disabilities

US Business Leadership Network

- The Business Leadership Network (BLN) was originally established in 1994 through the President's Committee on Employment with People with Disabilities (PCEPD — a small federal agency whose chair and vice chairs were appointed by the President) with a national business advisory board chaired by Tom Donohue, the President of the US Chamber of Commerce.

- The Network was created through various Governors' and Mayor's' committees on disability and based on the premise that business responds to their peers. It underscores the idea that employers should be recognized as valued customers of the vocational rehabilitation system.

- After ODEP was created, business leaders within the BLN affiliates met at the annual national conference and voted to establish a national organization known as the US Business Leadership Network.

- The creation of the national organization was intended to assist the development and growth of affiliates across the U.S.

- In 2004, the USBLN affiliates elected representatives from affiliates across the U.S. to serve as the first USBLN Board of Directors.

- In 2010, the USBLN launched its *Biz2Biz Report newsletter*.

Outreach and Communication

- Providing expertise in developing information on the advancement of employment of people with disabilities and in communicating such information (e.g., print and electronic media, electronic assistance tools and ODEP's and the USBLN's websites) to employers

- Speaking, exhibiting, or appearing at ODEP or USBLN events

- Collaborating with other alliance participants on employer issues that are identified through the Alliance Program. The goal of the program is to help employers solve issues around the employment and retention of persons with disabilities.

Technical Assistance

- Identifying activities that demonstrate, evaluate or replicate model disability employment strategies

- Identifying employer-specific issues of concern to which the Alliance should direct particular attention and resources

- Promoting ODEP-funded technical assistance services, such as the Job Accommodation Network and the Employer Assistance and Resource Network

National Dialogue

- Raising awareness of and demonstrating their own commitment to the advancement of employment for people with disabilities whenever USBLN leaders address groups

- Developing and disseminating case studies illustrating the business value of employing people with disabilities and publicizing their results

- As appropriate, convening or participating in forums, roundtable discussions, or stakeholder meetings on employer leadership issues to help forge innovative solutions in the workplace on recruiting, hiring, retaining and promoting people with disabilities.[37]

---

[37] http://www.dol.gov/odep/alliances/usbln2.htm

"It is society's role to take reasonable steps to support you in your employment, but it is fairly and squarely your responsibility to advance your own career. Always keep up to date with technology and ensure that you get good technology training. Diversity in the workplace helps promote diversity in thinking in an organization in general and you are a resource to the organization to turn that into products and services that are usable by, and thus sellable to, a larger proportion of the public. Diversity is not just a moral good or a legal requirement; it is a secret weapon for success."

Gerry Ellis, CEO of Feel The BenefIT and Technical Specialist at Bank of Ireland

Disability Employment Quotas

Many governments have legislated employment quotas or goals to encourage employment of persons with disabilities. Goals are less restrictive than quotas but often have reporting and metrics associated with them. Quotas are often tied to government-imposed penalties for failure to comply. The presence of those quotas in any given country requires employers to implement specific processes.

Some countries have found that despite the efforts of quota programs the employment outcomes for people with disabilities have not shown significant improvement. It was interesting to analyze those quota patterns. The countries that had the best results with quota legislation were those which deployed substantial programs to facilitate the hiring of persons with disabilities including providing services to employers such as Spain or France.

However, there is a risk that quota programs may accidentally send the message that the person with a disability was only employed because the company wished to reach its quota and not because they were qualified to do the job.

The table below lists the countries currently legislating quotas, and the type of quota they use.

Countries using Quotas

Australia

All public- and private-sector employers are subject to a quota of 4 percent of an undertaking's workforce. The quota law requires employers with more than 24 employees to employ one registered person with disabilities per 25 employees.

Austria

The Disabled Persons Employment Act (BeinstG), which includes a 4 percent quota scheme. Employers with a minimum of 25 employees must employ one registered persons with disabilities per 25 employees.

China

Employers must reserve no less than 1.5 percent of all job opportunities for persons with disabilities and employers who fail to comply with the quota must pay a fine to a Disabled Persons' Employment Security Fund.

France

Employers having a total workforce of more than 20 employees must ensure that at least 6 percent of their personnel are workers with disabilities. Said quota is based upon the actual percentage of population among 15 to 65 years old living with disabilities and eligible to receive support from the government. If employers do not meet the quota obligation, they must make an annual contribution to a fund for the vocational integration of people with disabilities. This contribution is proportional to the gap between the actual numbers of employees with disabilities compared to the theoretical level of 6 percent of their workforce. As of 2012, 41percent of French employers reached or exceeded the 6 percent quota of employment of persons with disabilities. And today, fewer than half of French employers pay a fine for failing to reach their quota, including only 8 percent that have no focus at all on employing persons with disabilities.

Germany

Employers of more than 20 people have quotas of 5 percent for the employment of people with profound levels of disability.

Greece

The 5 percent quota system applies to other groups of people seen as deserving an income from employment, such as war invalids, members of the family of persons with disabilities, as well as parents in families with many children and ex-members of the national resistance.

India

Indian employers are required to reserve up to 3 percent of positions for people with disabilities.

Ireland

Ireland has a 3 percent this quota which they call a target for the employment of people with disabilities in the public and civil service. This quota, which they prefer to call a target, has figured in social partnership agreements and is supported in the current 2004 Disability Legislation Consultation Group proposals to government. The Irish National Disability Authority (NDA) conducted a research project to investigate potential methods for measuring compliance with the 3 percent target for the employment of persons with disabilities in public bodies.[38]

Italy

---

[38]   http://www.inis.gov.ie/website/nda/cntmgmtnew.nsf/0/ 84AA79B029E870AE8025729D0046CAED/$File/people_with_ disabilities_in_public_sector_04.htm

Employers have an employment quota of 7 percent for people with disabilities. They also have penalties for non-compliance. The groups of people with disabilities that can qualify for the quota: civil invalids, work invalids, invalids of war and people with sensory impairments.

Japan

Employers have a 1.8 percent quota for employment of people with disabilities with a penalty for failure to comply is a monthly fine of 50,000 yen.

Luxembourg

Employers have a 5 percent employment quota for both the public and private sector.

Netherlands

The Employment of Handicapped Workers Act went into effect in 1986 and established a quota of 5 percent employment of people with disabilities.

Oman

The Ministry of Social Development (MoSD) stipulates that 2 percent of total posts in government offices should be reserved for the disabled. The rule for the private sector states that any establishment with a staff of more than 50 is encouraged to hire candidates with disabilities.

Portugal

Public administration had a 5 percent quota introduced in 2000. This quota is specifically geared to people with disabilities or with cerebral paralysis with a degree of incapacity equal to or higher than 60 percent, as defined by the country. Some countries attempt to define what it means to have a disability based on perceived percentage incapacity.

Spain

Employers with over 50 employees have a 2 percent quota for people with disabilities.

United States

The U.S. Department of Labor's Office of Federal Contract Compliance Programs (OFCCP) created regulations to establish a nationwide 7 percent utilization goal for qualified individuals with disabilities (IWDs). Federal contractors apply the goal to each of their job groups or to their entire workforce if the contractor has 100 or fewer employees.

United Kingdom (UK)

The United Kingdom abandoned its quota system in 1995 and instead enacted legislation making it unlawful to discriminate against people with disabilities in the employment relationship.

Bottom line:

Persons with disabilities present a unique solution to many of the current skill gap facing employers in the global economy, and while government-funded services to assist them in hiring employees with disabilities seem effective, quota legislation alone does not help corporate efforts at inclusion.

Business Perspective: Emily Ladau, Employee with Disabilities

"I urge employers to look beyond stereotypes and realize that employees with disabilities can be assets to a business. How? Simple: We're just like everyone else. Just as potential employees who do not identify as disabled bring unique skills and experiences to a job, so too will people with disabilities. It is so important for employers to remember that having a disability makes a person neither a superhero nor a tragedy.

So, please don't hire me:

- *If you are looking for an office mascot or a beacon of inspiration.*

- *If you see me as little more than a community service project.*

- *You think the sight of the poor employee in the wheelchair might help you close a deal.*

- *If I will be nothing more than a token of diversity.*

Hire me because you believe I'm the best person for the job." Emily Ladau [39]

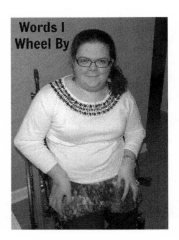

Emily Ladau

---

[39] *http://wordsiwheelby.com/*

Business Perspective:
SOGETI - France

SOGETI: Talent is All

Interview by Christine Leblois

"Sogeti is interested in exceptional talent, and disability does not impact talent." In a few words, Michiel Boreel, chief technology officer of Sogeti, defines the philosophy of the group. With more than 20,000 specialists around the world, Sogeti is among the leading providers in technology and software testing, specializing in application, infrastructure and engineering services.

"Most of our people are knowledge workers, qualified by a good working brain, and in this age of client-centric services, we strive to bring to our customers the best possible experience, with the best possible team."

Technology creates a more level playing field for workers of all abilities, and Sogeti leverages it on several levels. The group applies the W3C and WCAG standards in their products and services for accessibility, it provides training and promotes awareness in the engineers' teams to create a favorable working environment for persons with disabilities, and it encourages discussion around disability and employment through various initiatives, notably Defi H, one of Sogeti's programs.

"We train our engineers in security and privacy issues. Adding accessibility to those technology questions broadens enormously the type of products and services that can be offered on the market," says Boreel.

He adds, "Technology is becoming empathic, and those systems become almost like prosthetics to our brains. The interconnection of all these tools radically changes the landscape, and this is very good news for persons with disabilities. We do not need to optimize the processors any more, we need to optimize the tools, and define specialized devices for specialized tasks. The only limit now is the creativity of the human brain."

Progress in technology has led to a raising awareness for digital accessibility, and the corporate social responsibility policy at Sogeti follows that trend.

These efforts are also a response to legal obligations, as Bruno Dumas, head of human resources at Sogeti France, points out: French law requires that 6 percent of the workforce be persons with disabilities. This is a challenging proposition in the information technology field, according to Dumas.

Presently, around 2 percent of Sogeti France workers are persons with disabilities, four times the average in the industry. But, "our major customers do not necessarily think in those terms, and many applications are defined without including accessibility features," says Dumas

Sogeti puts accessible software and products in place internally to provide a more flexible environment. But the major obstacle is recruitment: "We can't find enough persons with disabilities with the right background in French engineering schools. Over the last 10 years, the aura of computer technology education has diminished, and students privilege prefer other fields in education than the regular computer engineering."

Sogeti works closely with the three rehabilitation centers in France to promote computer engineering, but according to Dumas, education should start at the high school level for students with disabilities. The group has launched a number of initiatives with associations and higher education institutions, as well as public organizations, and hopes those efforts will, in the long term, raise awareness of the potential of employment for persons with disabilities and create a major talent pool among them.

DEFI H: BRING THE COMMUNITY TOGETHER

The year 2014 saw the third annual Défi H competition. Launched by Sogeti in 2011, co-branded with Le MonInformatique.fr, the top ranking site in France for IT professionals, and in partnership with four main French nonprofit associations (Tremplin, L'Adapt, Execo and La Fondation de Garches), Defi H has three principles: open the discussion around disability and employment, promote innovation and the entrepreneurial spirit, and push forward education in computer engineering and technology.

Championed by Jacques Mezhrahid, director of innovation at Sogeti France, Défi H organizes teams of four students from higher education engineering institutions, paired with a disabled person's organization, to develop projects that promote employment for persons with disabilities. Those projects must have a practical application, like reeducation for the hearing impaired, or geolocation for the visually impaired.

Seven teams competed in the 2014 Defi H, with the support of Sogeti engineers, whom they met with once a month. Throughout the development of the project, each team's reporter kept the flow of publicity going, following editorial rules and using social media like Facebook and Twitter, to provide information for the widest possible audience and to exchange comments, questions and answers on technical issues. A jury reviewed the projects, including the impact of the social media effort (the "likes" will bring bonus points), and the selected teams presented to a panel before choosing the winner.

Defi H has become more important since the first competition in 2012. In 2014, 60 higher education institutions were partners of the project in France. "There is no mercantile objective for Sogeti, no marketing benefits," Mezhrahid says of the project. "Defi H is centered on students and persons with disabilities. This challenge is about bringing the community together, and bringing something to the community."

Chapter 4
Blending Disability Inclusion into the Organization

"If you believe in the human capabilities, anything is possible. People with disabilities can contribute to the economic system, but employers need to think creatively in order to unleash the capabilities of their employees, including people with disabilities. By having a job, I can live independently, contribute meaningfully to the workforce, pursue my dreams, fall in love, and anything is possible."

Jack Brandt, Disability Policy
Specialist, Virginia Partnership
for People with Disabilities

The Roadmap

To ensure the enterprise can be successful with all the moving parts of the organization, it needs to create a roadmap to implement disability inclusion. The roadmap helps blend accessibility into its processes, track progress and measure results. The roadmap should include a plan with deliverables, timelines, and metrics.

In fact, disability inclusion and accessibility initiatives can be risky without a plan. This is primarily because it may be subject to departmental interpretations and adjustments across diverse organizations. To be sure that the enterprise is pursuing inclusion in a legal and consistent manner, it needs to put time, thought, and funding into evaluating its current practices and planning how it will adjust them.

Many organizations benefit by working with accessibility and disability inclusion strategists. A seasoned professional can help a firm create a solid plan of attack.

Business Perspective: TD BANK

TD Bank, headquartered in Canada, has established a working system to identify and address accessibility issues in its organization, as it describes on its website:

"We understood that we needed to consult with experts; those that work on a daily basis to remove barriers for people with disabilities. That's why we established a group of community organizations to consult with regard to our planning and programs. The

group – with representation from Canadian organizations that champion the needs of people with disabilities – provided feedback on TD Bank's accessibility practices and identified areas for improvement."[40]

TD Bank of Canada found that marketing to customers with disabilities opened their company up to many different segments of the market they had not previously considered:

TD Bank in Canada is one company that has successfully implemented customer service accessibility practices. How did they do it?

"[We] listen – through customer experience surveys, focus groups, and talking with members of the community – and some of what we've implemented are:

- *Accessibility training for all customer-facing employees to educate them about TD Bank Accessibility services, and on properly serving all customers, including those with disabilities*

---

[40] https://www.tdcanadatrust.com/customer-service/accessibility/our-commitment-to-accessibility/index.jsp

- *Research on universal design to better understand how we can support people of all abilities*

- *Accessibility standards for our premise design and IT development"*

"In 2005, TD Bank had an entire program we had created about being an inclusive bank, not only for people with disabilities, but for other groups like aboriginal groups and visible minorities. ... TD Bank has many customers, and the census tells us that there are millions of people with disabilities in North America. So we understood that we had employees and customers with disabilities that needed access. TD Bank is committed to our employees and customers and we wanted to assure that we were providing inclusive [services] for everyone." [41]

[41] https://www.tdcanadatrust.com/customer-service/accessibility/our-commitment-to-accessibility/index.jsp

Here are a few ideas to include in a roadmap and how to expand policies:

1. **Vision/mission statement**

   a. Blend inclusion of persons with disabilities right into the company's vision/mission statement.

   b. Specify that the company is committed to full inclusion and the integration of accessible design for employees. Be sure to blend this commitment into every phase of the business, including employment, product design, policies and procedures, procurement, supply chain, and every department/function (e.g., human resources, financial, operations, corporate social responsibility or citizenship, training, and marketing).

   c. Try not to implement accessibility by creating separate technology or business processes; instead, mainstream accessibility in all technology and business processes.

4. **Diversity programs** are often viewed as a bridge between the workplace and the marketplace.

   e. When creating employment policies and programs, such as Equal Employment Opportunity or affirmative action policies in the United States, include disability, inclusion and accessibility components.

f. The programs should be owned by line organization, in addition to human resources. Be sure to include accountability mechanisms that require reporting to the Board of Directors, CEO, chief risk or compliance officer, and human resources.

7. **Recruitment policies and practices** should reflect a commitment to accessibility in this stage of employment, including the use of accessible e-recruiting tools and accommodation policies for interviews.

8. **Retention and disability inclusion management and prevention programs.** Create programs that allow employees to remain part of the workforce in the case of temporary or permanent disabilities. This allows an employer to keep experienced workers' intellectual capital and avoid retraining and the expense of replacing talented employees.

9. **Awareness and training on disability.** Expand base of knowledge and experience about disability inclusion and accessibility for all employees through various strategies such as through training sessions, demonstrations, newsletters. Best results in promoting disability inclusion are obtained with required training of all employees on an annual basis. Thereby allowing this process to be a sustainable practice that then becomes a core element of the corporate culture of the company.

10. **Procurement policies.** Adopt criteria for the purchase and use of information and communication technology (ICT) that is accessible and usable; this is sometimes referred to as universal design. This policy has many benefits, including increased productivity, reduction in the time it takes for employees to transition between systems, reduction in training, remediation and repurposing. The policy also helps reduce risks to the firm, since it allows all employees to use the new system, product, or tools and helps comply with legal requirements such as Section 508 in the United States.

11. **Promote the company's achievements in disability inclusion and accessibility as a "differentiator".** Applicants, employees, and customers are increasingly seeking accessible information and communication technology. Showing a company commitment to disability inclusion, accessibility and universal design standards and governance helps position it as an "employer of choice," which also resonates with the general public.

12. **Supply chain policies.** Consider expanding your supplier diversity programs to include businesses that are 51 percent or more owned, operated, controlled, and managed by individual(s) with disabilities.

13. **Communication policies.** Ensuring marketing, communications, and websites are fully accessible, on both the Internet and a company's intranet sides.

14. **Product development.** Build, implement, and manage accessible products and services.

15. **Telecommuting programs.** If the company has a telecommuting program, use it to accommodate schedules of employees with disabilities including the flexibility to work from home or at other remote sites away from the office, such as on the road or at a telework center.

16. **Employee Resource Groups or Affinity group.** Establish and support an Employee Resource Group for employees with disabilities and their families. Such networks facilitate communications between employees to share initiatives, ideas, accommodation solutions, and best practices. These groups can also help managers overcome resistance to creating accessible and inclusive business policies and practices. They can also help identify policies and practices that need to be addressed, as well as expand and improve how the company does business with its customers from a disability perspective.

17. **Designation of authority-centralized responsibility and source of information.** It will help to designate one contact point in a department whose responsibility it is to ensure consistent focus and resources are provided to employees on disability inclusion. This responsibility should include the development, implementation and

evaluation of accessibility and usability (universal design) initiatives.

18. **Cross-functional communications and coordination.** Formalize team approach. (e.g., accessibility team comprised of managers across divisions such as human resources, facilities, information and communication technology, procurement, education and training, financial, and every aspect of your internal and external corporate marketing).

19. **Internships/mentoring/shadowing programs** provide equal opportunities for individuals with disabilities to participate in company programs.

Human Resource Processes

Human resources (HR) has to carry the most critical part of these efforts. Inclusion of individuals with disabilities must be considered during each phase of the HR Recruiting and Employee Life Cycle. Each phase of the cycle must blend in disability inclusion and accessibility.

Human Resources recruiters must create, implement and manage an overall recruiting plan that outlines the type of candidates needed and how they will be reached. This plan must include processes to accommodate and include individuals with disabilities. All steps must be considered, including HR systems, internal and external communications, job descriptions, training, and online and career centers.

HR Employee Life Cycle

- **Recruitment:** The recruitment and applicant screening process must be updated to provide effective outreach to individuals with disabilities. For example, it is critical that employers minimize barriers in the application and screening processes. Can the candidate access the online application system and submit their resume? Can a candidate with a disability ask for an accommodation during the interview process? The entire process from disability outreach, company marketing, website, position descriptions, recruitment process, and policies must be considered.

- **Selection:** Train Recruiters, HR Staff, and Hiring Managers on tips to interview persons with disabilities, ask appropriate questions, and accommodate requests for candidates.

- **Induction/Onboarding:** Ensure all employees, including individuals with disabilities, are effectively and efficiently introduced to the organization. This includes introduction to their new positions, relevant policies and procedures, training programs, systems and processes of the organization.

- **Job Descriptions:** Properly prepared job descriptions are critical in effective performance management. Accurate job descriptions are a tool to effectively recruit and retain good employees, including individuals with disabilities. Job descriptions are a roadmap for recruiters, interviewers, managers, supervisors, applicants, and employees throughout the employment process.

- **Performance:** Be sure to focus on performance vs. the disability. Managers should have a performance standard for supporting and accommodating employees with disabilities. It is critical to provide coaching and mentorship opportunities and create processes that allow employees to effectively engage and retain employees with disabilities.

- **Training:** Training in issues related to persons with disabilities is important at all levels of the organization, from the C Suite to HR to operations. Useful training topics include disability awareness and sensitivity training, nondiscrimination in disciplinary or termination processes, nondiscriminatory recruitment and hiring practices, defining essential job functions, new hire orientation, the accommodation process, and accessibility.

- **Advancement:** Ensure that individuals with disabilities are encouraged to apply for promotions and that internal upward mobility is practiced for all employees. Often employees with disabilities are not given the same promotional opportunities as employees without disabilities. Opportunities for advancement should be made available to all employees, and facilities and training approaches must be examined to ensure accessibility for employees with disabilities.

- **Development:** All training programs, educational opportunities, and internal learning programs should be accessible for everyone, including employees with disabilities. Are websites or print training announcements accessible to persons with sensory impairments? Are training facilities wheelchair-accessible, and are training materials available in alternate formats (i.e., large print, CD/DVD, flash drive, audiotape, and/or Braille)?

- **Grievance Process:** Employees with disabilities need to understand the grievance procedures and responsible resolution of issues. Having an internal mechanism for resolving disputes is critical to an organization.

- **Retention:** Including employees with disabilities in retention plans helps an employer improve outcomes and differentiate themselves from other employers. Today's employees are looking for a career package that includes culture, career path, diversity of responsibilities, work/life balance, and corporate social responsibility.

- **Return to Work Programs:** An organization's workforce is its most valuable asset. When an employee can't work due to disability, illness or injury, the return-to-work process provides resources to assist in getting him or her back on the job quickly and smoothly taking into account his/her specific needs.

- **Transition:** Policies and practices for layoff, severance, retirement, etc., should be written and practiced consistently for all employees, including people with disabilities. Grievance layoff, termination, and discharge processes should be examined to ensure that individuals with disabilities are not disparately treated in these processes.

- **Accommodation:** It is imperative that the entire team is aware of their organization's disability inclusion and accommodation decision-making process. These programs lend themselves to increasing awareness of the importance of confidentiality, acceptance of individuals with disabilities in the workplace, and supervisor awareness of reasonable accommodation requirements, along with creating an organizational structure for those accommodations.

- **Budget procedures:** Best results in hiring employees with disabilities are obtained when the business unit does not hesitate to carry additional costs for accommodation. For this reason, major corporations typically create a companywide accommodation budget that provides funds for all assistive technologies and related devices and services not charged back to business units.

Impact of Accommodations on the Bottom Line

Many employers are confused about the cost of individual accommodations. Employers understand that they have to provide accommodations, but often they overestimate the cost, assuming that people with disabilities depend on expensive aids that will not work with their systems. Those misperceptions create artificial barriers that can prevent individuals with disabilities from being hired or retained to perform jobs they could do with accommodations.

Reasonable accommodations remove workplace barriers for individuals with disabilities. They allow individuals with disabilities to perform their jobs and be as productive as their peers without disabilities. The good news is that job accommodations, in general, are reasonably priced.

According to the U.S. Department of Labor, Job Accommodations Network annual report, *Workplace Accommodations: Low Cost, High Impact,* "workplace accommodations not only are low cost, but also positively impact the workplace in many ways." [42] Employers reported that providing accommodations resulted in retaining valuable employees, improving productivity and morale, reducing workers' compensation and training costs, and improving company diversity. The report found that accommodations had an average cost of $500. How much is that cost compared to the cost of employee turnover? It is clearly much less expensive to provide the accommodation than to have an employee leave and have to recruit and train someone new.

Some barriers, however, may be the result of inaccessible legacy infrastructure and costly to retrofit. They may include

---

[42] www.askjan.org

physical obstacles (inaccessible facilities, bathrooms or equipment), or inaccessible systems (inaccessible intranet, HR systems or enterprise-wide systems). Hence the importance of applying procurement processes that ensure that all infrastructure investments provide adequate accessibility.

It is worth noting that accommodations are not just about employing individuals with disabilities. Employers accommodate employees every day by trying to treat employees fairly and equitably. The goal is not to treat everyone exactly the same, but to consider what the employee needs and to understand that employees' needs change over time.

Enterprise Execution

We covered HR, now let's look at the rest of the organization. From the board of directors, CEO, and chief risk officer to HR, to the marketing area, all the way through operations and production, each part of the organization has a role to play.

> *"The 'tone at the top' as demonstrated by the board of directors and executive management is especially important as an organization implements changes ensuring individuals with disabilities are assimilated into the workforce. The board must monitor the progress and success of implementation efforts undertaken*

by executive management and front line business units.

"Monitoring of such efforts is often conducted and reported by a chief compliance officer and/or a chief risk officer and internal audits. Accountability for implementation must also be baked into individual employee job performance standards. As with any initiative involving major change, the board of directors must ensure it clearly explains why the initiative is being pursued, what the end game is, and how progress will be assessed."

Robert Lane, former national bank examiner,
Office of the Comptroller of the Currency,
President, Lane Risk Consulting, LLC

Measure - Mitigate Risk

Risk mitigation remains a key concern of employers in relation to the employment of persons with disabilities, especially in those countries with a strong litigation culture. The most effective way to reduce risk is to create and implement a comprehensive disability inclusion plan or roadmap as described above. While compliance should not be the driving factor to promote the employment of persons with disabilities, it is important to make all management levels of the organization aware of the potential liabilities that can result from missteps in the recruitment, management or termination of employees with disabilities.

C Suite and Board of Directors

The Board of Directors and C Suite have important roles to play in the ongoing success of a company's disability inclusion efforts. These teams oversee all of the Company's business and affairs and should be committed to a strong corporate governance structures, diverse workforce, risk management and business practices that help the company achieve the best results. The board and C Suite is also responsible for the effectiveness of public policy, legal and political compliance, and social programs. A study completed by Korn Ferry showed that 96 percent of executives believed that a diverse and inclusive workforce led to improved business results and higher employee engagement. "We are encouraged that executives recognize that having a diverse and inclusive workplace gives them a strategic advantage in the marketplace," says Oris Stuart, a senior partner at Korn Ferry Leadership and Talent Consulting. "At the same time, there's work to do in holding managers and leaders accountable and creating incentives." Over 400 executives participated in the diversity and inclusion study. [43]

---

[43] http://www.cioinsight.com/it-management/workplace/slideshows/how-diversity-delivers-on-roi-employee-engagement.html

Information Technology and Communications

Accessible technology tools on the job are an essential aspect of accommodation for employees with disabilities. Without those, essential tasks cannot be performed. It is therefore extremely important that managers of information systems understand the common problems encountered by employees with disabilities. Most potential issues, if not all, can be eliminated or improved upon by proper communications and training of information systems staff that interact with employees with disabilities. There are numerous solutions that allow people with disabilities to easily navigate ICT systems and applications.

Any enterprise-wide and department systems must be accessible to everyone, including employees with disabilities. Whenever information systems are procured, they must be selected with accessibility criteria in mind. Whenever they are revamped, upgraded and revised, they must remain accessible. Quality assurance, quality control and testing should include accessibility metrics. There are many moving parts in the ICT areas: it is therefore important to include ICT accessibility in all technology roadmaps alongside criteria such as privacy, security or ease of use. Areas should include all employee and customer touchpoints, including:

- Company website

- Intranet

- HR systems

- Customer service systems

- Employee meetings

- Training (Instructor-led and online)

- Kiosks

- Company applications and software programs

- Documents and PDFs

- Enterprise systems

- Division systems

- Department systems

- Telecommunication systems

- Internal and external communications and marketing

- Help desks

- Technical support

Bottom line: Any ICT that is used in the organization should be accessible by all employees. Accessibility efforts also make other systems and services more accessible and usable for employees without disabilities. For example, training has been created for persons with disabilities and instead of only using text, the employer explained the process via graphs and pictures. That training allows the employer to onboard future employees with and without disabilities quicker and more efficiently.

Marketing and Communications

Marketing can help an organization capitalize on new market opportunities. So it is important that programs mirror the market to attract a wider customer base. All marketing and communications should be accessible. For example, internal communications bulletins should be accessible to all employees. Corporate announcements should be accessible. Some of my clients have created video announcements from the leadership team and captioned those videos to allow all employees to benefit from the message, including those who are multitasking or for whom English is their second language. Also, consider using models with disabilities in your advertising and marketing brochures. Many firms focus on a diverse population in their marketing campaigns but forget to include people with disabilities.

Customer Service

Customer service must be accessible to employees and customers with disabilities. All call centers, technical support areas and communication should be fully accessible.

Customer service representatives should also be trained on how to accommodate and serve people with disabilities. Call centers should be capable of fielding inquiries via TTY and e-mail, as well as phone, fax, virtual messaging (text, IM) and regular mail. In addition, an accessibility call handling procedure should be put in place to ensure that every effort is made to accommodate your customers with disabilities by immediately escalating inquiries that are not successfully concluded on the initial contact.

Beyond these specialized adjustments, the key to providing quality services to customers with disabilities is to remember that all customers are individuals. Persons with disabilities come in all shapes and sizes, with diverse personalities, abilities, interests, needs, and preferences – just like every other customer. Etiquette considered appropriate when interacting with customers with disabilities is based primarily on respect and courtesy. Representatives should listen and learn from what the customer tells them regarding their needs. Remember, customers with disabilities will continue to engage with and support businesses that welcome them, are helpful and accessible and provide quality services.

Representatives should rely on common sense to guide interactions with people with disabilities and behave in the same courteous and respectful way with individuals with disabilities that they would with anyone.

Procurement

All procurements should include language that ensures that products and services purchased are accessible. This is a critical step because if a company is procuring inaccessible services or products from their vendors, it adds considerable risks and costs to the company. Often an organization forgets to add procurement language requiring the vendor(s) to comply with accessibility laws or standards. Only after the company begins to implement the system, it realizes that employees with disabilities cannot access it. If procurement forgot to add accessibility language as part of the requirements, the firm will have to retrofit the system, typically a very costly endeavor.

Accessibility language should be part of the criteria for procurement acquisition. The language does not have to be extensive. For ICT products, for instance, language can say that all ICT systems and products must comply with W3C WCAG 2.0 AA standards[44] or U.S.[45] or European public procurement standards[46] for ICT accessibility. This is critical across the board, but especially for enterprise-level systems or technologies that affect a large number

---

[44] http://www.w3.org/WAI/

[45] http://www.section508.gov/

[46] http://www.google.com/url?sa=t&rct=j&q=&esrc=s&source=web&cd=2&cad=rja&uact=8&ved=0CCYQFjABahUKEwjkIt7I5sfHAhWBSj4KHWLkCJ8&url=http%3A%2F%2Fwww.etsi.org%2Fdeliver%2Fetsi_en%2F301500_301599%2F3

of employees. Considering accessibility in procurement involves the following steps:

1. Vendors should be asked to provide information about the accessibility of their products.

2. The information provided by vendors must be valid, measured using a method that is reliable and objective. For example, many companies will use a Voluntary Product Accessibility Template (VPAT). The VPAT was created by industry so that the U.S. government could compare one vendor's accessibility efforts with another's. You can learn more about VPATs at www.section508.gov.

3. Procurement officers should be trained so they can objectively evaluate the information provided by the participating vendors as well as the accessibility of the products they are selling. Many vendors offer training for their clients, and free training is available on www.section508.gov and www.access-board.gov.

Supply Chain

Another area to consider is the supply chain. This does not affect the employees, but using vendors that are owned by persons with disabilities is considered a best practice. There are programs that certify entrepreneurs with disabilities. One such program is in the United States and run by the US Business Leadership Network (USBLN).

The US Business Leadership Network Disability Supplier Diversity Program (USBLN DSDP) offers businesses that are owned by individuals with a disability, including service-disabled veterans, the option to be certified. Such certification helps these business owners to access potential contracting opportunities with major corporations, government agencies, and one another.

For more information: http://www.usbln.org/dsdp_overview.html

Bottom line: Incorporating persons with disabilities into your workforce is not only a matter of hiring and accommodation. It requires an companywide commitment to creating a culture that welcomes and understands the perspective of persons with disabilities.

Business Perspective: CANON

Canon's leadership in promoting the employment of persons with disabilities

In an age of increasing internationalization and diversification of societal needs, making effective use of the strengths and individuality of a diverse workforce is more important than ever. For this reason, Canon makes special efforts to respect the rights of each and every employee and to build a corporate culture that fosters diversity.

Promoting Employment of Persons with Disabilities

Respecting the ideal of normalization as advocated by the United Nations, Canon actively employs persons with disabilities.

To ensure a comfortable workplace for all, in addition to improvements to facilities, such as greater barrier-free access, Canon Inc. holds hearings to review departments where employees with disabilities have been assigned.

Canon plans to continue such initiatives so as to expand employment opportunities for persons living with disabilities.[47]

---

[47] http://www.canon.com/csr/report/pdf/canon-sus-2015-e.pdf

Canon Wind, a special subsidiary of Oita Canon dedicated to increasing employment opportunities and the range of job duties for persons with disabilities

Canon has blended accessibility into their global products.

Through universal design, accessibility and inclusion, our goal is to create products and services that provide every customer with a sense of emotional attachment and excitement in every situation. In recent years, our customer base in advanced countries has become increasingly diverse, even as the populations of these countries grow increasingly mature.

"In order for a company to grow continuously, it is essential that employees, who are the life force of a company's operations, be provided with a comfortable work environment and that their talents are fully utilized. At Canon, we offer skills training support and fair treatment to our employees. In addition, we give due consideration to promoting a healthy work-life balance and ensuring occupational health and safety, enabling our employees to work in security and with peace of mind.

With operations throughout the world, Canon currently employs over 190,000 people.

Paul Albano, senior manager, Enterprises Solutions Marketing, Canon USA

Chapter 5
Tying It All Together

"New information and communications technologies can improve the quality of life for people with disabilities, but only if such technologies are designed from the beginning so that everyone can use them. Given the explosive growth in the use of the World Wide Web for publishing, electronic commerce, lifelong learning and the delivery of government services, it is vital that the Web be accessible to everyone."

U.S. President Bill Clinton, April 4, 1997[48]

Hiring and retaining employees with disabilities is no different from hiring and retaining other employees. All employees need accommodations from time to time, and as mentioned earlier, most accommodations are inexpensive or have no cost attached. These efforts are about ensuring all employees feel valued in the workforce and are productive.

---

[48] http://thinkexist.com/quotation/new_information_and_ communications_technologies/337057.html

Employees Lives Change

It is also important to note that employees' needs change all the time. As employees walk their life journey, they experience changes along the path. Employees may experience many and sometimes all of these paths as they work for your firm:

- Acquire a temporary or permanent disability due to many factors including accidents, illness or age related problems

- Need to support aging parents or relatives

- Have a spouse or loved one who needs temporary or long-term support due to disabilities

> *"People with disabilities who are leaders in business are critical to opening the nation's eyes to the incredible talents of people with disabilities. For example, Virgin Airways founder Sir Richard Branson and finance wizard Charles Schwab are dyslexic. Scientist Stephen Hawking, Governor Greg Abbott of Texas, and President Franklin D. Roosevelt are/were wheelchair users. Another example is, Steve Wynn. Wynn's name is synonymous with glittering and opulent towers, high stakes, and business success. Wynn is vision impaired because of retinitis pigmentosa. In 2013, the casino magnate and billionaire donated $25*

million to further research into this disease and other conditions that cause vision loss."

Jennifer Laszlo Mizrah, CEO
of RespectAbility

All world-class employers understand that to keep their talented employees and attract the top talent, they need to be flexible and supportive. Disabilities are part of life, so ensuring that your workforce is fully accommodated allows employees to be productive, happy and innovative. *"Happiness makes people 12 percent more productive, and generating that happiness can be as simple as taking the time to hear out their thoughts."*[49]

Employers are always focusing on ways to keep up with competition. Including employees with disabilities in your workforce is one way to achieve these goals. Employees with disabilities can help drive innovation into the core of your processes. Studies have shown that employees with disabilities are loyal, productive team members.

"A study[50] by the Institute for Corporate Productivity (i4cp), which surveys and analyzes the practices of high-performing businesses, found that one of the reasons employers proactively hire people with disabilities is that

---

[49] http://www.foxnews.com/us/2015/10/14/how-to-inspire-innovation-among-employees/

[50] http://www.imintohire.org/download-the-report/

it supports their corporate culture. As the report states, this positive impact "is brought about in two ways: [it] adds highly motivated people to the workforce (which can lead to increased productivity) and it promotes an inclusive culture that appeals to the talent pool organizations want to attract." That's a win-win!"

Mark Perriello, President & CEO
Kauai Chamber of Commerce,
Former CEO of AAPD

Business Perspective:
ENTERPRISE RENT-A-CAR

Part of the largest rental car group in the world, Enterprise Rent-A-Car has been actively exploring ways to incorporate people with learning disabilities across all parts of the business for a number of years. The company's EMEA HR director, Donna Miller, describes this as a "journey – a learning journey".

Established in 1957 by Jack Taylor, and still owned by the Taylor family, Enterprise embodies diversity as a core strategy for building a talented and loyal workforce. The company recruits graduates at the entry level and then only promotes from within: a talent pipeline is a vital resource to ensure the quality of future leadership. A number of systems, structures and processes are used to ensure that recognition and promotion is in line with the founding principles of the company. Alongside a focus on customer service, responsibility for employee development and community service, promoting diversity is drilled into every individual in the company and is fundamental to employee reviews and promotions.

"Of course diversity is part of doing the right thing," continues Miller. "But it has commercial benefits and it has done wonders for both staff and customer engagement."

If the "why" of hiring people with learning disabilities is straightforward, Miller admits the "how" and the "what" can be more complicated. "When it comes to learning disability, doing the right thing can be hard to establish. Mencap's Disability Confident scheme helps us to define the best way to integrate people with learning disabilities into our business. We are also working with Great With Disability. Being awarded the 'two ticks positive-about-disability 'symbol gives us confidence that we are doing the right things when it comes to attracting and retaining people with disabilities."

Senior level Enterprise directors act as sponsors for driving action through the business. In fact, one of the more recent drivers for greater focus on empowering employees with learning disabilities was when a senior manager's cancer treatment began to affect his cognitive abilities.

This sponsorship is vital in ensuring simple decisions can be made to avoid wasting resources on systems and equipment which may not be really beneficial. Enterprise engages with experts to avoid making basic mistakes. The company works closely with the Business Disability Forum and also has a disability sub-committee to the overall diversity group which meets every month to discuss new and existing initiatives and improvements.

This includes streamlining the reasonable adjustment procedure to make it quicker for employees to get the products, services, and equipment they need, researching software to provide better experience and access for people with disabilities and looking at job specifications and home-working arrangements.

On a practical level, Enterprise works with individuals on a one-to-one level to find the best fit with their needs and their ambitions. This can mean a completely bespoke approach or slightly tailoring an existing arrangement. Miller emphasizes that this "is no different to how we might approach any employee who may have specific needs in order to be their best".

There can be hidden benefits. "Who knew that tools such as software which can read back email and website copy can be really useful for those colleagues who don't speak English as a first language? As a rapidly growing international business with operations in almost every part of the globe, this software is proving to be really useful on many levels."

Engaging existing employees with what is changing is also a vital step. "In the UK we are over 4500 people working at well over 400 locations. Initiatives such as the Accessible Technology Charter, which documents our commitment to provide accessible technology for our customers and employees, Mencap's Disability Confident, and the International Day of the Disabled Person help raise awareness with our existing employees. We want everyone to know what we are doing so that people engage with the fact that creating the environment where people with learning disabilities can thrive benefits everyone."

At the heart of Enterprise commitment to diversity is a belief in its role in building a strong culture. "Some of our diversity initiatives do not appear to be directly related to work. It seems a stretch to say that taking a group of employees to watch films that have all been made or produced by disabled individuals helps us to be better managers, leaders and employees or that it helps us to be better at renting cars. But it does; we have seen it happen. When we grow as individuals, when we develop our understanding for what can be achieved, we help to build a stronger culture where everyone can contribute, work better, and be more successful."

Employer Opportunity

Modern technology and communications have changed the way we work, and our approach to employment has also changed. Designing and delivering internal and external accessible Internet, communications and technology (ICT) adds value to employees with and without disabilities. It also benefits a company's clients when products and services are developed and designed with the client's experience in mind.

Adopting Universal Design strategies will keep an organization ahead of the curve in the areas of legal compliance, reduced risk to its brand and corporate social responsibility – a win-win for everyone. Ultimately, Universal Design and ICT Accessibility efforts make services and products more usable for all employees and customers – not only individuals with disabilities.

Accessibility is the degree to which the ICT environment is available to all employees, customers, vendors and other stakeholders. Accessibility allows employees with disabilities the ability to access internal ICT systems and services. Accessible ICT allows employees who use assistive technology to be as productive as other employees.

"Innovation occurs at the intersection of invention and insight. It's about the application of invention — the fusion of new developments and new approaches to solve problems. Accessibility is one area where you can harness insight into what makes your organization productive, and steer inventions that are essential to meeting standards and enhancing user experience — to arrive at innovation."

Frances West, IBM, Chief Accessibility Officer

Universal Design supports accessibility when something can be used "out of the box" by employees with different abilities, or when something is compatible with various adaptive and assistive technologies. Universally designed technology benefits the majority of employees. As an example, accessible web pages are often easier to read, easier to navigate, and faster to download, and they also improve the search engine optimization (SEO) ranking.

Both accessible and inclusive design promotes innovations that help employees with disabilities as well as often benefiting your clients and other stakeholders.

> *"Self-confidence is a tool that will bring one a long way. Always try to keep up to date with technology and ensure that you get good technology training. Assistive technologies are far more sophisticated than in the past and can interoperate more easily with mainstream technologies. These can ease the burden of gaining access to information such as company policies and activities. They can even give the user an advantage over other people who need to use technology but are not confident with its use."*

> Gerry Ellis, CEO of Feel The BenefIT and
> Technical Specialist at Bank of Ireland

Captioning is one example. Originally created for people who are deaf or hearing loss, captioning also allows employees that cannot hear your corporate videos to read the captions – an important innovation, since televisions are now located in offices, airports, train stations, gyms, corporate cafeterias, and many other venues where background noise may make listening a challenge.

Companies that address accessibility needs by adopting Universal Design principles will be better positioned to leverage those same Universal Design principles for their entire customer base.

> *"Accessibility is about enabling human ability to break down barriers to ALL people."*

Frances West, IBM, Chief Accessibility Officer.

Article by Gartner Inc. estimates that the worldwide population of persons with disabilities and their immediate family control $8 trillion dollars in discretionary income. Gartner estimates that by 2050, 30 percent of the population of 64 countries will be older than 60 and many of those people will benefit from assistive technologies and accessible ICT.[51]

Employers are learning that supporting employees with disabilities can add benefit to the rest of their workforce.

---

[51] http://www.gartner.com/newsroom/id/2638315

Many technological advancements have been created for and by persons with disabilities.

―――――――――――――――――――

Business Perspective:
ROYAL CARIBBEAN INTERNATIONAL

An interview with **Ron Pettit, Royal Caribbean Cruises Ltd**, ADA & Access Compliance Consultant, Trade Support & Service

Royal Caribbean ACCESSIBILITY ONBOARD

"There's a wonderful world of adventure awaiting you and there's no one that can bring it to life like Royal Caribbean International®. We've always believed that discovering and exploring the world around us is something that everyone should be able to enjoy, and over the years we've been an industry leader in providing the finest cruise vacation experience for all of our guests."[52]

We often say it's not just a vacation, it's about making memories. I really enjoy helping people with disabilities create unique memories - special moments in their lives that they can't

―――――――――――

[52] http://www.royalcaribbean.com/allaboutcruising/accessibleseas/home.do

get on land. There's something about the cruise experience that is truly magical - being on the water, the unique onboard experience we have on our ships - that makes a wonderful setting for people with disabilities to make shared memories that last a lifetime.

I love working at Royal Caribbean. One of the reasons I came to Royal Caribbean is because I knew they were and continue to be an industry leader in providing accessible cruise vacations. I wanted to work for a cruise line that was the best cruise line for people with disabilities, and help them reach that next level. I've been here for 10 years (my tenth anniversary will be in April), and we have had many great accomplishments:

- Hosted two full ship charters for deaf and hard of hearing guests (in 2007 on Freedom of the Seas - 3,800 guests and 2014 on Jewel of the Seas - 2,300 guests)

- Became the first ever Autism Friendly Cruise Line (Royal Caribbean International in 2014 and Celebrity Cruises in 2015)

- Initiated only one but three advisory boards on disabilities - Guest Advisory Board on Disabilities, Autism Advisory Board and

Accessible Travel Agent Advisory Board (all in 2015)

Worked very closely with Newbuild to develop accessibility for three classes of ships - Oasis and Quantum class (for Royal Caribbean International) and Solstice class (for Celebrity Cruises)

To learn more about Royal Caribbean's commitment to employees and guest with disabilities, visit. http://www.royalcaribbean.com/allaboutcruising/accessibleseas/home.do

Employment and Universal Design

"In the late 90's I began to see a pattern. Once I recruited persons with disabilities as I built capacity, safety ratings increased, absenteeism dropped, staff morale peaked and, most importantly, turnover dropped dramatically. I noticed that although for obvious reasons, staff with disabilities did not leave, those without disabilities left at a much lower rate, too, than at my Tim Hortons colleagues locations – 35 percent, versus [the] 100 percent norm for the industry – and this is a clear economic benefit. Hiring people

with disabilities often doesn't require adding accommodation measures and can boost the profit of a business."

Mark Wafer, Megleen, President and
Tim Hortons, Toronto Franchisee

Remember, when you create an accessible environment that allows qualified candidates with disabilities to compete for employment, you broaden your talent pool and drive in qualified candidates to meet your hiring needs. Improved access via Universal Design can expand choices of jobs for applicants with disabilities and also create opportunities for current team members with and without disabilities.

As Tim Hortons discusses in the quote above, your firm's effectiveness can be seriously impacted by the expense of recruiting and hiring, combined with the disruption of turnover and staffing shortages. Creating an accessible and universally designed work environment will allow your organization to retain its valuable knowledge base by allowing aging workers to remain on the job with sustained satisfaction and productivity.

Accessible tools and infrastructure can also benefit employees without disabilities. According to a study commissioned by Microsoft, 57 percent of working-age adults in the U.S. (more than 100 million) are likely to benefit from using accessible technology.[53] The study showed that many people with mild disabilities benefited from the use of assistive technology. Many of these employees do not identify as having an accessibility, accommodation or disability issue; nevertheless, their difficulties cause productivity issues. Those challenges can be resolved by accessible ICT solutions.

Business Perspective: EY

An interview with Lori Golden, Abilities Strategy Leader, EY

EY's flexible work environment is the single best tool we have to support our people with differing abilities. Both informal and formal flexibility enables people with chronic health conditions or those recovering from illnesses or treatments to continue to do their jobs and better manage their lives.

We integrate ergonomics and accessibility into our offices, technologies, tools and business processes. In addition, we educate our people about diverse abilities, raise awareness of non-visible disabilities such as chronic health

---

[53] "Accessible Technology in Computing—Examining Awareness, Use, and Future Potential," A Research Report Commissioned by Microsoft Corporation and Conducted by Forrester Research, Inc., 2004.

conditions, illnesses and mental health issues, and train on topics like disabilities-friendly etiquette, language and work habits.

It is our aim to foster an understanding that all of us have a range of abilities and at times, disabilities, both long-term and temporary, such as complications of pregnancy, injuries and recovery after surgery.

Some of our achievements at EY include:

- Sponsoring the Career Opportunities for Students with Disabilities national conference and recruiting events and participating in the Emerging Leaders intern program to help build the pipeline of talented college graduates with disabilities

- Serving on the US Business Leadership Network's Board of Directors, participating in the U.S. Department of Labor's Circle of Champions, serving on the Advisory Boards for the American Association of People with Disabilities/US Business Leadership Network Disability Equality Index and America's Disability Rights Museum on Wheels.

- Helping found the National Business and Disabilities Council's Accommodations Think Tank and the Financial Services Abilities Roundtable

- Sponsoring the first Learning Disabilities in the Workplace Forum, where employers, universities, people with disabilities and specialists discussed how companies can better support employees with learning disabilities

- Hosting the Business Taskforce on Accessible Technology/ National Business and Disability Council CIO Accessibility Forum[54]

Starting with our founder, Arthur Young, we have always embraced differing abilities. Trained as a lawyer, Arthur was deaf with low vision, and he wasn't able to comfortably practice. He turned to finance and the new field of accounting to build his career. His "disability" drove him to innovation and

---

[54] http://www.ey.com/US/en/About-us/Our-people-and-culture/ Diversity-and-inclusiveness/Unleashing-our-full-abilities--1-- Making-a-difference

entrepreneurship, which played a pivotal role in the development of our firm. [55]

═══════════════════════════════

When internal systems are made accessible, it is easier for employees without disabilities to learn to use those systems, saving time on training and making employees more productive.

Companies spend a lot of money on technology in the hope it will improve employee efficiency and drive down costs. When accessibility is blended into the lifecycle of the technology implementation or procurement process, it improves these business processes, in addition to increasing productivity, eliminating waste, enhancing customer service, maximizing effectiveness of employees, and reducing labor costs.

Technology plays an important role in business, and new technology has emerged as a prime component for allowing business to meet their strategic goals. Now consider that 10 percent to 20 percent of your customers cannot access your technology solutions because of accessibility issues. Gartner forecasted nearly $3.7 trillion would be spent on technology worldwide in 2014. If your customers and employees cannot access your technological solutions the cost to the organization are staggering.[56]

---

[55] http://www.ey.com/US/en/About-us/Our-people-and-culture/Diversity-and-inclusiveness/Unleashing-our-full-abilities--1--Making-a-difference

[56] www.gartner.com

Remember, accessibility allows as many people as possible to use technology solutions, which include services, products, tools, devices, or other ICT environments.

> *"Underlying the legal and practical realities of the 'information age' is the recognition of the vast capacity of accessible technology to unlock human potential, to tap into great reservoirs of intellect and ability that have gone largely untapped until now, and to maximize productivity and performance for all."*
>
> John Kemp, CEO, The Viscardi Center

Summary

"Ultimately, we must learn as a society to look past the physical and allow the mental strengths and prowess of this group to be tapped into when looking for positions that lack the requirement of physical aptitude. Companies can only flourish and show strength in leadership amongst their peers by being proactive with this movement. The vast human capital of the PwD community is just waiting to be tapped into and given the opportunity to contribute their underutilized talents to the corporate world and society in general."

Richard J. Streitz, Ruh Global Communications, Chief Operating Officer, Former Disney Imagineer

Employees with disabilities are like every other employee. There is no mystery to successfully employing persons with disabilities. Employers all over the world are successfully hiring and retaining employees with disabilities. Remember, disabilities may be a part of the life journey for many of your employees. When you create solid policies, standards and processes to successfully employ and retain persons with disabilities, everyone wins.

Employers that focus on each of their employee's abilities instead of their disabilities will win each time. Additionally, as the global marketplace continues to demand that persons with disabilities be included in all aspects of society, your firm will reap the benefits of full inclusion.

Companies of all sizes are trying to figure out how to assure the public that they are socially responsible corporations. Hiring a diverse workforce that includes talented persons with disabilities is one way to accomplish your goals. Hiring individuals with disabilities in your workforce makes good business sense and adds value to your bottom line.

Employers invest a lot in their human capital. Invest in human capital that includes and accommodates employees with disabilities and you will be able to tap into a creative, loyal, productive and diverse workforce.

"No pessimist ever discovered the secret of the stars, or sailed to an uncharted land, or opened a new doorway for the human spirit."

Helen Keller[57]

---

[57] http://www.brainyquote.com/quotes/quotes/h/helenkelle161286.html

Made in the USA
Columbia, SC
16 August 2020